THEY CALL ME DOC

(An autobiography, characteristics of good teaching, it happened in the classroom, and educational issues for anyone who wants to be a teacher or just wants to know something about teachers and teaching)

By

Ken Riggs

Contents

Introduction 5
Acknowledgements 9
Biographical Information 11
Section One 13
   Autobiographical 13
     I Remember..14
     More Open Doors 30
Section Two..35
   Characteristics of a good Teacher............................36
   Effective Bible Teaching..47
   Teaching Attributes Personified...............................54
Section Three 69
   It Happened in the Classroom 70
Section Four 87
   Educational Issues...88
     The Christian and the Public Schools 89
     Christianity and Psychology................................ 109
     Self-Concept and Children 116
Closing Comments 137

Ken Riggs

Copyright 2011
By
Ken Riggs

ISBN   Soft cover 978-0-9829070-6-1

All rights reserved
No part of this book may be reproduced or transmitted in any form or by any means, electronic or mechanical, including photocopying, recording, or by any information storage and retrieval system, without permission in writing from the copyright owner.

All Scripture verses are from the KJV

This book was printed in the United States of America.

To order additional copies of this book, contact:
Ken Riggs
3829 Hwy 49-W
Springfield, TN 37172
Kennethriggs2001@hotmail.com

FWB

Printed by FWB Publications

They Call Me Doc

Introduction

Another book about teaching! Big deal. Yes, it is another book about teaching, and, no, it's not a big deal. It's just something I wanted to do. My entire adult life has been in the classroom. I've taught at every level from elementary school through college. It has been a fantastic journey, and I'm still doing it. I don't want to forget the journey. If along the way you, the reader, glean something from it, it will have been more than worth my time. I do need to confess something to you. It is not a typical book about teaching. It's a book about my experiences; it's a book about what I think makes a good teacher. It's a book of practicality.

I have chosen to put my remarks in sections for organizational purposes. The first section is more like an autobiography. It's about the steps I took to become a teacher. The second section contains my own thoughts about what I think are the characteristics of a good teacher. I will do that by showing five characteristics of the teaching ministry of Jesus Christ. If you are a believer, I offer His characteristics as a challenge to you. If you're not a believer, you will probably still agree that Jesus was one of the greatest teachers who ever lived.

The second thing I want to do concerning the characteristics of a good teacher is to present two essential characteristics of teaching but make the application to my love for teaching the Bible. You can make the adaptation to whatever you teach. The third thing I want to do in the section about the attributes of teachers is to tell you about some of the teachers I've been privileged to have who have left a tremendous impact on me as a person and as a teacher. Each of them will display a different characteristic that, again,

They Call Me Doc

every teacher should possess. This is my way of paying tribute to those people, although most of them I will not mention by name.

The third section, to me, is the most interesting. I want to share actual experiences that happened in the classroom. Some are humorous. Some are more serious. Every teacher knows what that's all about. I'm calling this section It Happened in the Classroom.

The fourth, and final, section was the most difficult to write, but I feel it must be included. I want to write about three educational issues I've had to face as a Christian teacher. I believe in Christian Education. At the same time, I firmly believe there is a place for the Christian in the public arena. Christian teachers are involved in Christian Education by virtue of the fact they're Christians. Granted, some Christians teach in private, religious schools while others teach in public schools. Two other issues will be presented, namely Christianity and psychology, how they are similar but most importantly, how they differ. The final issue will be developing an attitude of self-esteem in the lives of children.

If you are a teacher, or have been, you may see a little of yourself in this book. If you're thinking about becoming a teacher, I hope what I say here will help you along your journey. If you're not a teacher or never have been and have no desire to be one in the future, I think the book can still be entertaining.

Here it is. A book that is partially an autobiography of a teacher; a book that gives some of the attributes of a good teacher; a book that tells of some of the antics that have occurred in the classroom; and a book that seeks to analyze

They Call Me Doc

three educational issues that need to be understood. Autobiography of a teacher, attributes of good teaching, antics in the classroom, and an analysis of issues. Hopefully, you will remember something about the book, and then again, maybe not, but enjoy the book. I had a good time writing it.

Ken Riggs
March 2011

They Call Me Doc

Acknowledgements

The writing of any material for publication is never a one-man project. In my case that is certainly a fact. I wish I was able to personally contact every person for whom I am grateful, but unfortunately, that's not possible. I do want to thank all those teachers who have influenced my teaching. I have included them in one of the chapters dealing with the characteristics of good teachers. I want to thank the literally hundreds of students who have put up with my antics, sense of humor, and style of teaching.

A word of appreciation is due to Alton Loveless who guided me through the manuscript and publication process.

The former Dean of Free Will Baptist Bible College, and colleague, Dr. Robert Picirilli, was more than gracious to read the manuscript in its infancy and give me the benefit of his editorial expertise.

I am appreciative to Joy Corn, former student and colleague, for proof reading the final manuscript.

A heartfelt word of appreciation must be acknowledged to my family. My wife, Carolyn, has put up with me for over 50 years. In fact, she helped me through one undergraduate degree, two master's degrees, and one doctorate. When I completed my doctorate degree from Peabody/Vanderbilt in 1978, we had been married sixteen years. She said, "Ken, we've been married sixteen years; you've been in college twelve of those years. Isn't that enough?" I agreed. Thanks honey, for all your patience and help.

They Call Me Doc

My three sons, Jeff, Kevin, and Jonathan are the joy of my life. I have said before, but it needs to be stated here, I knew parents could spoil their kids, but I didn't realize kids could spoil their parents. Ours have spoiled us.

To have three sons who faithfully serve the Lord is more than any parent could hope for. I love each of you and your families!

They Call Me Doc

Biographical Information

Dr. Ken Riggs has been an ordained Free Will Baptist minister since 1963. His ministry and career have been spent as an educator. He served as the principal of the first established Christian School in the Free Will Baptist denomination which was founded by his father, the late Rev. Raymond Riggs. He served on the faculty of Free Will Baptist Bible College from 1971-1993. Most of that time was as the Chairman of the Teacher Education program. He served as the Administrator of Pleasant View Christian School in Pleasant View, Tennessee from 2004-2010. Since 1991 he has served, and continues to serve as an Adjunct Professor for the Nashville State Community College in the field of Psychology. He has authored a variety of materials, namely, two gospel tracts, "Fight Than Switch," and "Four Letter Words"; three booklets, "You Can Know," a booklet explaining the assurance of salvation, "How To Live Right," a booklet explaining how to use biblical principles in deciding between right and wrong, and "The Runaway," the story of his personal conversion, and a book on the life of his father, "By The Way...,".

As a minister, he has conducted many youth revivals, family seminars, and teacher education workshops for Sunday school teachers. He has served as an interim pastor of several Free Will Baptist churches in the Nashville, Tennessee area. For almost ten years he served as the Senior Pastor of the West Meade Fellowship, an interdenominational church, in the Bellevue area of Nashville.

They Call Me Doc

He has written a variety of articles for the former <u>Contact</u> Magazine, and now <u>ONE</u> Magazine, the official magazine of the Free Will Baptist denomination. He and his wife, Carolyn, have been married since 1962. They have three married sons, Jeff and Sherry, Kevin and Misty, and Jonathan and Lara and are the grandparents of ten grandchildren. Ken and Carolyn reside in the state of Tennessee, in the Nashville area.

SECTION ONE

Autobiographical
I Remember
More Open Doors

They Call Me Doc

I Remember

I don't remember when I decided I wanted to be a teacher. I have always liked school. Even as a child, I enjoyed going to school. My earliest memories are in the elementary grades. At the time, I lived with my parents in Highland Park, Michigan. I went to Robert E. Barber Elementary School. We lived about ten or twelve blocks from there. Most of the time, I walked to school. Other times one of my parents would take me or I would catch a ride with a neighbor who was going that way. I remember one time I walked but forgot how to get there so I turned around and went back home and hid under the bed until I thought school would be out. In those days you went home for lunch and came back to school after you had eaten. Those were the days when you could advance or fail a half of year instead a full year.

I remember being selected to be a "pick-up-boy." That was a boy who had been chosen to pick up trash around the school. You were given a stick with a nail at the end of it so you could use the stick to pick up the trash and put it in a bag. I'm not sure how I got chosen, but I remember you were made to feel special for being selected. I got promoted from a pick-up-boy to safety patrol. A safety patrol was a boy who got to wear a white belt that crisscrossed over your chest. Your job was to stand on the corner to be sure it was safe for others to cross the street. I had a friend who was a higher patrol than I was. He got to wear a badge on his belt that said he had been appointed to be a Lieutenant.

I remember in elementary school drawing pictures of

They Call Me Doc

the Detroit waterfront, although I never went there much. I remember having a crush on a teacher in my sixth grade. She was a very attractive tall Greek lady with coal black hair. I wasn't the only boy in the class with a crush on her. One of my friends liked her, too. I remember another teacher who taught Social Studies. She made us learn the map of the United States. She would give us a blank map and we had to fill in all the states. After that we had to learn the capitals of each of the states. This was back when there were only 48 states, but I remember when Hawaii and Alaska became part of the United States.

One of the memories I do not like was elementary gym classes. The teacher would appoint two captains and they would choose who they wanted to be on their teams to play whatever sport was in season. I was seldom chosen, or at least not first. Most of the time I was chosen last or sometimes the teacher would tell me what team to be on. I liked sports but was not really good at any of them. However, I do remember the gym teacher showing me how to get the ball to go through the rim when we played basketball. The backboard had two black marks in the shape of an X, one on each side of the rim of the basket. The teacher said if you would hit either one of those marks at a slight angle, you would make the goal. He was right. His taking just a small amount of time to show me left a deep impression on my mind.

It's hard for some people who think they really know me to believe it, but in elementary and even in high school, I was rather shy and withdrawn. There were several reasons for that. Physically, I was pigeon-toed to the point that I had to wear corrective shoes. The heels of my shoes were higher

They Call Me Doc

on one side than the other. This forced my feet to turn outward in an attempt to make me walk straight. My teeth were perfectly white but they were crooked with two of the front teeth protruding that looked like fangs. Consequently I was often called names like "fang face" or just plain "fang." Added to that was the fact I spoke with a very pronounced lisp. The lisp made my speech very sloppy. That is, when I talked saliva would often drool from my mouth. I was in a speech therapy class quite often. I later learned that I had an oversized tongue that was actually too large for my mouth. My teeth did not meet properly so when I talked, air would escape between my teeth causing the lisp. Pigeon-toed, ugly teeth and a lisp don't make you very popular. In fact I was often laughed at.

In my teen years there was another aspect that added to my shyness. I was a "preacher's kid." This really became an issue when my family moved to Tennessee and I entered junior high and high school. When I was twelve years old, my dad made the decision for the family to move. All I had ever known was living in the Detroit area. I had only gone to one church, the Highland Park Free Will Baptist Church. My dad was the pastor and my mother was the organist. I was confused about the move. I didn't understand the reason for leaving family and friends to move somewhere else. The move simply added another problem to the ones I already had. Get the picture: pigeon-toed, ugly teeth, a lisp, and now I'm a Yankee with a northern accent living in the south. Talking made matters worse. Believe me this is a lot for a boy of any age to have on his psychological plate.

The year was 1953. I enrolled in what was then Richland Elementary School on Charlotte Pike in West

They Call Me Doc

Nashville. It was an elementary school with grades one to eight. I was in the seventh grade. Academically, I had no problem. Socially was another issue. I did not realize it then, but as I look back it was another teacher that showed an interest in me that became a tremendous influence. He had the same name as a well known country artist, but he was a Church of Christ preacher who was the physical education teacher and coach. The school had no gym. All gym classes were held outside on an asphalt slab when the weather was appropriate. A small softball diamond was situated behind one of the buildings. Other parts of the school ground had swings and places to just run around.

I remember the day the coach announced there would be tryouts for the basketball team. I had tried my hand at organized sports only one time before. That was when I tried to play baseball when I lived in Michigan, but I was too frightened by the ball when I batted to really be a good player. In Tennessee I did have a basketball goal on a telephone pole in our backyard. Two friends from the neighborhood had goals in their backyards as well and I would play with them so I thought I had nothing to lose in trying out for the team.

I really don't know how it happened, but the coach chose me to be one of the members of the team. He had chosen twelve boys. Our school colors were green and white. I was given a uniform with the number 55 on the jersey. We practiced outside on the asphalt court but played our games in the surrounding schools that had gyms. I was what I called the sixth man on a five man team. I was usually one of the first substitutes to be put in the game. I don't ever remember actually being a "starter," but I played in almost every game.

They Call Me Doc

When I was promoted to the eighth grade, I made the team again.

I remember the day the coach asked the members of the team if any of our parents could help transport us to the games. I asked my mother, and she volunteered and ended up going to almost all the games. She did more than drive us. She bought each member of the team a white towel and knitted two great big green letters on it. The letters were RR which stood for "Richland Rockets."

Richland Elementary School was in the city limits, but I lived farther out in the county. I was able to ride a school bus as far as it would go towards the county line, but then I'd have to walk the rest of the way home. During basketball season, I was unable to ride the bus so I would often just walk all the way home. After completing the eighth grade, I had to decide where I would go to high school. I had two choices: the school in the city which was Cohn High School or the county school which was Bellevue High School. It was my choice. My older brother had chosen to go to Bellevue. I didn't know where I would go.

An eighth grade teacher at Richland Elementary School had a husband who was the coach at Cohn High School, the city school. He had seen me play for Richland Elementary School and knew I had the choice to attend either a county or city school. He encouraged me to come to Cohn and play for him. Since he took an interest in me, and I didn't know anybody at Bellevue, I told him I would. I guess you could say I was recruited! Cohn was not just a high school. It had grades seventh through twelve with grades seven through nine being considered junior high and grades ten through

They Call Me Doc

twelve being high school.

I played ball on the junior high team in the ninth grade. In the tenth grade I made the B team for the high school varsity team. The B team would play games prior to the varsity team, and then sometimes I would get to dress out in a varsity uniform and sit on the bench during the varsity games. A few times I even got to play in a varsity game as a sophomore. That was a thrill!

My education at Cohn was a good one. As I look back over those days, I realize just how good an education I did receive. To this day I can still remember many of my teachers and most of my classmates, particularly those in my Senior Class. Not everything I learned was academic. This was in the days when the culture was family oriented and moral, at least by today's standards. Our high school assembly programs had a short devotion. The high school chaplain, who had been elected by the student body, would read from the Bible and pray.

It wasn't all calm, however. I remember the day some boys threw cherry bombs in the commodes on the third floor, and I remember when a boy was stabbed in the hallway. I remember when some boys ran a truck off a hill into the home of the principal who lived nearby. I remember a "dummy" that was hung in the auditorium with the name of the assistant principal on it and a knife stuck in his chest. Because of these events, the Metro Nashville Police were called in to patrol the halls for a few days.

I was encouraged to join the Future Teachers of America (FTA), and was selected to be part of the Key Club which

They Call Me Doc

was sponsored by the local Civitan Club. Long after I graduated from Cohn, I saw some of my teachers from time to time and they remembered me. They would ask about me. I graduated in 1959, and to this day many of my classmates still get together for reunions or communicate through e-mail. Not long ago we celebrated our fiftieth anniversary. The class sponsor who had been with us from grades nine through twelve, attended. In fact, when I took the position as Administrator of Pleasant View Christian School in 2004, I received a letter from her stating how proud she was of me and that she would be praying for me.

When I graduated from high school, I fully intended to go to college. In fact, I wanted to attend George Peabody College for Teachers in Nashville, Tennessee. However, I got a job instead, left home, and thought I was going to get married. (That's another story you can read in a booklet I've written entitled "The Runaway"). In the spring of 1960 I decided to enroll for the fall semester at Free Will Baptist Bible College which was the college sponsored by the denomination in which I had been raised. I had known about this college for a long time but never really thought about attending. It had no programs of study to prepare you to be a school teacher, but I decided to attend anyway.

Quite by surprise, I received a phone call from the College Registrar, Dr. Robert Picirilli. He had learned that I was planning to attend that fall. He asked me if I would be interested in singing and traveling with a quartet for that summer. The quartet would travel to the churches of the denomination seeking to raise funds as well as recruit other young people in the denomination to attend college. I told him I would. Then he suggested I enroll, if possible, in

They Call Me Doc

summer school to take at least a class or two. I agreed to do so. I don't know all the history of the college, but I may have been one of the only people to be in the college quartet before actually being a student.

Even though there were only a few courses to take that would prepare me to be a teacher, I took as many as were offered. During my four years as a student, I kept thinking about being a teacher. I suggested to some it would be a good idea to add a teaching program to the curriculum. It may have been discussed with those who make decisions but I didn't hear any more about it until a few years later.

I married my wife, Carolyn Rutledge, in the summer of 1962 and continued my education at Free Will Baptist Bible College. I was employed by another agency within my denomination that produced literature for what was known as Church Training Service (CTS). It was similar to Sunday school except it met on Sunday nights. It was a program that included all ages, but concentrated on children and young people. I did a variety of things such as work in the mailing room and fill curriculum requests for churches throughout the United States and teach seminars for Sunday school teachers in local churches. I also served as National Youth Evangelist under the auspices of the Church Training Service Department.

This experience proved to be valuable in preparing me to be a teacher. My boss, Mr. Sam Johnson, who had been a school teacher previously, was the director of the CTS department along with his wife, Jane. Between the three of us, and occasionally other temporary help, the work was completed. The both of them had a tremendous impact on

They Call Me Doc

me. They taught me the value of doing what is right even in the face of criticism. When I graduated in 1964, I still wanted to be a teacher, but I was faced with a problem. My degree from Free Will Baptist Bible College did not permit me to apply for licensure as a teacher so I continued to work for two more years.

I started to enroll in Bob Jones University in Greenville, South Carolina, which was much larger and had a teacher education program. I was accepted and even planned to move and enroll for the fall semester of 1966 when I received a phone call from my dad. He was the pastor of Bethany Free Will Baptist Church in Norfolk, Virginia, and was planning to begin the first private Christian school in our denomination. I had never heard of, nor seen, such a school.

Because I was doing some preaching at the time, my dad asked me to come and conduct some services for him, but in reality, he wanted to convince me I needed to come and work with him. He had been a school teacher in the old one-room school house type and knew I was interested in teaching. During that week we talked about the school the church was planning to start. What my dad was doing was making history for our denomination. No other church had begun a school as yet. This was to be the first one. I knew nothing about school work, but my dad was very persistent. I told him I had already made plans to go to graduate school in the fall.

Daddy suggested I check out a public, state operated college which was in Norfolk, Old Dominion University. I told him I didn't think that would work because my degree was from a religious, and to some, a non-accredited college.

They Call Me Doc

He insisted I check it out. Quite frankly, to satisfy him I made an appointment with the Director of Admissions and told him of my interest in becoming a certified teacher. I told him about my degree from Free Will Baptist Bible College which he had never heard of. However, he did agree to think about it a couple of days and asked me to call him before I was to leave town. I assured him I would.

My wife and I continued making plans to move to South Carolina. I called the Director of Admissions of Old Dominion, and to my amazement I was going to be accepted for the fall semester if I wanted to come. I couldn't believe it! I was being accepted with a non-accredited degree without having to make up any credits. I took this as a confirmation from the Lord that I should cancel my plans for graduate school and move to Norfolk instead. Not long after that, my wife and two little boys, Jeff and Kevin, moved. For the next three years, from 1966-1969, I served the church of which my father was pastor. My responsibilities were to be the Principal of the school, teach the second and third grades, and be the Music and Youth Director for the church. In addition to that, I started taking graduate classes at Old Dominion.

It was a historical time, and sometimes even hectic. My father and I were making denominational history. He started the very first Christian school in our denomination and I served as the first principal. After three years, I completed my graduate courses but was not quite finished with my thesis, but we left Norfolk, Virginia, and moved to Knoxville, Tennessee, for a short time to live with my wife's parents. I did complete the work on the thesis and received a Master's Degree in early 1971.

They Call Me Doc

The years 1969-71 were a little difficult. I had returned to a preaching schedule as often as opportunities became available. Our oldest son, Jeff, was old enough to be in the first grade so I decided to home school him so the family could be together rather than be separated. We purchased a Holiday Rambler Trailer and as invitations came, we hit the road, pulling the trailer behind a Delta 88 Oldsmobile. That was our home. We would park in church parking lots where I was to preach and a few times we parked in campgrounds. The curriculum I chose to use with my son was a good one. It was a good curriculum in that I would present the material, he would do the work, and then I mailed everything to the curriculum's Home Office where a teacher was assigned to grade and correspond with our son. It was a good experience, but very hard and trying. After one year, I decided the family should settle down in Knoxville, Tennessee, while I continued to travel. That last year I was on the road, I was away from my family thirty-five out of fifty-two weeks.

While in Norfolk serving with my dad, I had been in touch with Dr. Charles Thigpen, the Dean of Free Will Baptist Bible College, about the possibility of becoming a faculty member. He had talked with me about coming to teach, with the intent of helping to establish a teacher education program and when he felt the timing was right, he would contact me. Early in 1971 my family and I moved to Nashville and I began teaching as a substitute teacher for the Metro Nashville Public Schools and occasionally substituted at some other private schools in the area. I had also enrolled to work on another Master's Degree at Middle Tennessee State University in Murfreesboro, Tennessee. Working as a substitute teacher does not pay a big salary and it was a

They Call Me Doc

struggle. One day the Treasurer of Free Will Baptist Bible College, Mr. E.B. McDonald, called to ask if I would be interested in working at night as a supervisor in the Library. I agreed to do so for the added income for my family.

I don't remember the exact date but I do remember the day Dr. Charles Thigpen, called to tell me he felt it was time for me to join the faculty of the college. I was still a graduate student, but the classes were on Saturday and that did not present a problem. I joined the faculty of the college in the fall of 1971. Two other men, Mr. Henry Oliver and Dr. Douglas Simpson, had already begun work on the teacher education program. Ironically, Dr. Simpson and I had been roommates as students. The three of us continued to work on the development of a teacher education program that would ultimately lead to full accreditation from the Tennessee State Department of Education and licensure for the graduates in the teacher education program. At the time the Registrar, Dr. Robert Picirilli, guided the three of us through the process with the State Department of Education. My responsibilities as a member of the teacher education faculty were to teach courses in the teacher education curriculum and be the Director of Student Teachers. For the first four or five years, the teacher education program continued, but full accreditation and licensure came later.

I'm not exactly sure when Dr. Picirilli suggested I should go to graduate school to earn a doctorate. I had never thought of that possibility. I was strongly encouraged to do so because the other two men with whom I had been working to develop the teacher education program had moved on. One had retired and one took another teaching position in another state. I was encouraged to find a suitable, and if possible, local college to attend. It was believed that another faculty member with a doctorate degree in education would be of benefit, particularly in seeking to be accredited by the Tennessee State Department of Education. One program that I considered was relatively new and was going to have a campus in the Nashville area. It was not a traditional program of graduate work. Classes would meet on weekends at a local college, but assignments would be done outside of class. I discussed this with Dr. Picirilli and both of us felt it was not a good choice.

It was decided that I should check out George Peabody College for Teachers. Remember, this was the college I wanted to attend after high school graduation. After the proper registration procedures, I was accepted as a student into the doctoral graduate program. I had already completed two graduate degrees, a Master's in Guidance and Counseling, and a Master's in Curriculum and Instruction. I thought it would be logical to enroll in Peabody's education program for the Doctor of Education degree, known as the Ed.D. I did that because I knew to enroll for the Ph.D. degree meant having to take a foreign language, which I didn't want to do.

I don't know if you're noticing a pattern in my educational career, but it was becoming very clear to me. Each step of the way I was being guided, sometimes without even realizing it. To have been accepted into a graduate program in Norfolk, Virginia, to have the opportunity to be a principal of an elementary school, to have the experience of home schooling one of my children, to be a substitute teacher in public schools of Nashville, to be a member of the faculty of Free Will Baptist Bible College, and now the possibility of attending the college I had wanted to attend in the first place,

They Call Me Doc

was sufficient confirmation that I was in the Lord's will. The biggest surprise was yet to come.

After one semester at Peabody, I received a call from the Dean of the graduate programs. His actual first name was Dean so he was known as Dean Dean. He had been going over my application and program of intent to graduate and noticed that I wanted to earn the Ed.D. degree. He was curious why I didn't want to get the Ph.D. He knew that Free Will Baptist Bible College was seeking approval for accreditation from the Tennessee State Department of Education and it was his opinion the Ph.D. would be better than the Ed.D. I told him I didn't want to take a foreign language so I chose the Ed.D. path. He said, "You've already had two years of a foreign language." I reminded him that my foreign language, which was Greek, was in my undergraduate program. He responded, "That doesn't make any difference. I'm changing your program of intent to the Ph.D. The Tennessee State Department of Education will like that better." He did not require me to take any proficiency tests or make up any work at all. With the stroke of a pen, he changed the degree. I graduated with the Ph.D. in Curriculum and Instruction in 1978. One of the first classes as a student at Peabody also gave me confirmation, or at least encouragement. As the teacher, Dr. Jack White, was calling the roll, he would ask students where they had attended college before. When he came to me, I responded that I had attended and graduated from Free Will Baptist Bible College and was a member of the faculty. To my surprise, he responded, "I attended there too." We had many conversations about students with whom he had attended and he became a constant source of encouragement to me. In fact, he became the Chairman of my Doctoral Dissertation

They Call Me Doc

Committee.

When it came time to make the decision regarding a dissertation, I was required to take a class in which you actually wrote a proposal as a part of the class assignment. I submitted a proposal entitled, "The Educational Philosophy of Robert Raikes." I had studied his life earlier and was interested in him. But that was not to be. The Chairman of my Dissertation Committee called me in his office and asked why I was writing a dissertation about Robert Raikes. I told him of my interest. He didn't like the idea and said something like this, "Ken, I know you have been working to help establish a teacher education program that will allow the college both of us attended to receive accreditation and licensure for graduates of the teacher education program. Why don't you write about that for your dissertation?" I could hardly believe what I was hearing. Truthfully, I wanted to do that but thought that would be turned down. Mr. Henry Oliver, Dr. Douglas Simpson, Dr. Robert Picirilli and I had invested many hours in writing proposals, surveying the denomination to discern their interest in having a teacher education program, talking to other like colleges who had teacher education programs, and countless other tasks that were involved. With the suggestion, and approval of Dr. White, I changed my complete dissertation

I must tell you one more experience while at Peabody that absolutely influenced my entire teaching career. When I enrolled as a student, I was given a list of all the classes that were to be taken for my intended program. I noticed that one of those was a class in statistics. I was horrified. I had a poor math background and was already dreading that class. I intentionally took it as my very last class. The first day of statistics my spirit, emotions, and confidence were lifted. The teacher began to explain how he would conduct the class, what we were to do, and what he expected. He said something like this, "I'm going to tell you what I want you to know; I'm going to show you want I want you to know and do; and then you're going to write some things down." Tell. Show. Write. With the aid of an overhead projector, an understandable lecture presentation, and a handout for every assignment, I learned statistics and passed the class. When I graduated, I went to him and personally thanked him for not only being a good teacher, but also showing me a method that I have since adopted as my own. I call it the three-in-one-method. I seldom teach a class of any kind without using an overhead projector, making things as clear as possible, and giving a handout of some kind.

I hope you have noticed the path of the sovereignty of God in my personal life. That's not meant to be an arrogant statement. It's meant to be praise to God. The Psalmist said, *"Commit thy way unto the Lord; trust also in him; and he shall bring it to pass"* (Psalm 37:5). *"The steps of a good man are ordered by the Lord; and he delighteth in his way"* (Psalm 37:23). I remember that as a young man of nineteen, when I committed my life to Christ, I promised to do His will. I have honestly sought to do nothing but that, and God has been faithful.

More Open Doors

From September 1971 until May 1993, I served on the Teacher Education faculty of Free Will Baptist Bible College. Much of that time was as the Chairman of the Teacher Education Faculty. Those were some of the best years of my life, and I can honestly say I do not regret any of the time. There were rough spots along the way, but all careers, jobs, and ministries have those. Little did I know that over the next sixteen years, three other opportunities of service would come my way. Leaving the Bible College did not end my teaching career. In fact, once again the sovereign hand of Lord was at work. At the beginning of the spring 1991 semester, I was in my office helping register students for their classes. I received a phone call from Dr. Sam Gant from Nashville State Community College. I had met him earlier but only chatted with him briefly. He told me a teacher had unexpectedly resigned and he needed a teacher. I told him I was busy with registration and I would get back with him at the end of the week. He said, "Classes begin tomorrow."

I told him that I would have to get clearance from Dr. Picirilli, my Dean, and would call him back later that day. I made an appointment to see Dr. Picirilli and explained the situation to him. The class I was being asked to teach was to be three days per week, during my scheduled lunch. I told Dr. Picirilli that with his permission I would miss my lunch those three days to help Dr. Gant. Dr. Picirilli agreed. That was in 1991. Since that time and even as this is being written (March 2011), I am still teaching for Nashville State Community College as an adjunct professor.

They Call Me Doc

When I retired from Free Will Baptist Bible College in 1993, I was also serving as the pastor of Sylvan Park Free Will Baptist Church on a part time basis. It was time to move on, so I resigned as pastor. A group of people with whom I had attended elementary and high school had begun a church in the Bellevue area where my family and I lived. I had preached for them on occasions while they were looking for a pastor. Most of them had been affiliated with the Cumberland Presbyterian Denomination. They approached me about being their pastor, but I said no. I thought doctrinal differences would be an issue, mainly the mode of baptism and perseverance of the saints (Calvinism versus Arminianism), but after discussions with them, I was elected as their pastor and served the church for almost ten years. They were gracious to let me continue my association as an adjunct professor.

When I left the pastorate in the fall of 2003, I really did not know where I would be going. For six months I had no employment, even though I faithfully applied and searched for another ministry or employment, but nothing became available. Then the opportunity came for me to join the staff of the Donelson Free Will Baptist Church. I had attended this church when my parents moved to Nashville in 1953. When I answered the call to preach, my very first sermon, October of 1961, was preached in what was then the basement sanctuary of this church. It seemed I had made a full circle. I was to become the Director of Adult Ministries and would be working under the pastoral leadership of a minister for whom I had, and still have, the highest regard and respect, Rev. Robert Morgan.

While I enjoyed the ministry at the Donelson Fellowship

They Call Me Doc

for the most part, I didn't feel satisfied or fulfilled. My love is education. One day Rob came into my office and said, "Ken, are you satisfied here?" I had to be honest so I told him I was not. I missed the classroom and during this brief time I was not teaching as an adjunct professor. I told him that if he didn't mind, I was going to begin looking for an educational opportunity that was more in line with my passion and desire. He was gracious and understood.

It was at this time that the position as Administrator of the Pleasant View Christian School became vacant and the Board of Directors was looking for a new administrator. I contacted them and we made arrangements for an interview. I had known about this school from its very beginning. My dad was not the founder of this school but he was serving the Good Springs Free Will Baptist Church in the Pleasant View area when the school was established in 1978. Classes actually met in the Good Springs Church. The Board of Directors told me they were only going to interview two candidates and make a decision between the two. I was one and a friend of mine, and a former student from my days at Free Will Baptist Bible College, was the other one. For whatever reasons, my friend was selected. I was disappointed not in him, but in the fact that I was not selected. I began looking for another position. Another Christian school in the Mt. Juliet area of Nashville was looking for an elementary principal so I contacted them and was asked to come for an interview. The interview went well and I was asked to come for a second interview to meet the members of the elementary school faculty. The date was arranged for that meeting.

Two days before the scheduled interview with this school in Mt. Juliet, a member of the Board of Directors

They Call Me Doc

from Pleasant View Christian School contacted me to inform me that my friend had decided not to come and they wanted to know if I was still interested. I informed him that since they had told me no, I was being interviewed for another position, but I would give it some thought. I did and decided to cancel the interview with the school in Mt. Juliet and accept the position with Pleasant View Christian School.

Of importance to my career as a teacher is the fact that the Board of Directors agreed for me to be a teaching administrator. That is, I requested to teach a class as well as serve as the administrator. Into my second year as the administrator I received a phone call from Nashville State Community College. They asked me to consider teaching for them under their program of Dual Enrollment. I didn't know what that was but quickly learned it was a program whereby qualified juniors and seniors in high school could take college courses and receive college credit while in high school. Dual Enrollment was soon launched as a part of the PVCS high school curriculum. Qualified students could earn a maximum of six semester hours of college credit by taking two courses, Introduction to Psychology and Human Growth and Development. These were the very courses I had been teaching since 1991. Get the picture: I'm being asked to teach college classes at Pleasant View Christian School in which I am serving as administrator and being paid by Nashville State for it.

I was delighted to be affiliated with Pleasant View Christian School for several reasons. First, it was a school with which my father had been affiliated. Second, many of the faculty and staff were former students of mine from Free Will Baptist Bible College. I had used PVCS as a place for

They Call Me Doc

student teachers. After six years of service, on July 31, 2010, I resigned as their administrator.

My first year of teaching was the fall of 1966. As this is being written, I'm still teaching. I'm in my forty-fifth year of teaching. My teaching experiences have taught me as much as I have tried to teach my students.

In closing this autobiographical section of my career, let me simply enumerate the ten most important things I have learned. I didn't learn these in a classroom before I began teaching; I learned them in the classroom as I taught.

- God opens doors that men think are shut.
- Follow what you believe is God's will even if it disagrees with others.
- You never know whom you will influence with both your life and knowledge.
- You will always learn something from your students.
- Every student is important, even the ones who don't make good grades.
- Students in both Christian College and other types of Christian schools are not always perfect; neither are their parents.
- People will disappoint you, but God won't.
- When you follow God, He already has His people where and when you need them.
- God has His people everywhere, regardless of their church affiliation, or lack of it.
- There are a lot of Christian students, teachers, and staff personnel in many public institutions.

Section Two

Characteristics of a Good Teacher
JESUS CHRIST: The Ultimate Educator
Effective Bible Teaching
Teaching Attributes Personified

Characteristics of a Good Teacher

If you have been in education very long, you soon learn there is a constant, on-going discussion about what constitutes good teaching. Scores of books have been written on the subject. By the time you finish reading one book, another one is on the market. That's probably not bad because good teachers understand that cultural climates do impact the style of teaching and knowledge.

In this section, I want to call attention to three things that illustrate what a good teacher is and consequently what good teaching is. I want to do this, first by presenting what I consider to be the ultimate educator, Jesus Christ. As a believer I have tried to discover what it was about Him that made Him such an outstanding teacher. I'm keenly aware that He had a distinct advantage over us. He was God in the flesh, and none of us will ever measure up to that standard, at least not in this life. But what was it, apart from His incarnation that attracted Him to others? I find it interesting that nowhere in the Scripture is Jesus referred to as a preacher. He is always referred to as a teacher. Different words are used, such as "taught", "teaching", etc., but never have I been able to find anywhere where He is called a preacher. That may be a moot point because in actuality there is a thin line between preaching and teaching. I used to tell my students the only difference I know in preaching and teaching is volume. If I get loud, I'm preaching. If I remain quiet, I'm teaching. My former college president, Dr. L. C. Johnson, used to say, "Every aspect of preaching should have an element of teaching." Then he would add, "Sometime in your classes, just preach."

They Call Me Doc

The second thing I want to point out involves two essential ingredients for every type of teaching situation. Because of my love to teach the Bible, I am going to illustrate those two essentials as they relate to teaching the Bible.

The third thing I want to do is list what I have discovered to be the most influential characteristics of a good teacher. Each characteristic was seen in the lives of the many individuals who crossed my path in my educational pursuit. I hope these three things will encourage you to continually strive to become the most influential teacher, or worker on the job, you can be.

JESUS CHRIST: The Ultimate Educator

You are probably familiar with the passage of scripture written in John 3:1-2. It reads:

"There was a man of the Pharisees, named Nicodemus, a ruler of the Jews. The same came to Jesus by night, and said unto him, Rabbi, we know that you are a teacher come from God: for no man can do these miracles that thou doest, except God be with him."

At this point I'm not concerned about Nicodemus and his being a Pharisee, a Rabbi, and coming to Jesus by night. I'm interested in what Nicodemus called Jesus: *"a teacher come from God."* I honestly wish I could remember where I read the following statement, but it was too long ago and I failed to write the reference down, but it expresses the sentiment that Jesus was definitely a teacher:

When Jesus was a teacher, it was His passion. He was not teaching when He wasn't doing something else, but when He wasn't doing something else, He was teaching. Teaching was His life.

I have read through the New Testament in search of what made Jesus such an outstanding teacher and have learned five things He constantly did. I have also read accounts of what secular history has said about Him and even though many unbelievers do not accept Jesus Christ as the Messiah, some of them do recognize He was a great teacher. Here are the five things I have learned about His teaching:

He Demonstrated What He Said

He was His own illustration. Whatever the topic, He illustrated it. He not only illustrated it, He personified it. That is probably one of the reasons His critics could find nothing wrong with Him. His language was seen in His life, or, as we would say He practiced what He preached. To illustrate this truth, note a few topics He taught and then continue the search on your own:

- Prayer, Matthew 26:36
- Obedience, Matthew 27:46, 47
- Submission to authority, Matthew 26:39
- Concern for parents, John 19:26; Luke 2:51
- Humility/Servanthood, John 13:14
- Forgiveness, Luke 23:34
- Love, John 15:12

One of the problems we often have in church settings is that some people talk one way but live another. Not so with Jesus. Even parents at times are guilty of saying one thing but doing another. Not Jesus.

They Call Me Doc

If you are a teacher, I can assure you that students watch you when you don't even know they're watching. It behooves us to be examples of our faith in the presence of others. The old adage that says, "Don't do as I do, do as I say" never has been a good idea. Jesus taught that we should be like Him. James says, *"Be ye doers of the word and not hearers only"* (James 1:22). James farther adds that to not be a doer not only deceives others, it actually deceives oneself. Even farther he says that believers should *"be a doer of the work"* (James 1:25). Jesus Christ certainly demonstrated what James states.

He Desired to Serve

I often said to students who were thinking about becoming a teacher, if you don't like kids, don't teach. It's not worth it and the money's not that good. My point was, and is: if you can't serve others, find something else to do besides teach. I think that applies to other areas as well. Jesus was a servant to others. He said, *"I didn't come for you to serve me: I came to serve you"* (Matthew 20:28). Look at his life. It was one of service to others. When you read the Scriptures listed above as to how Jesus demonstrated what He said, you see Him serving others.

He Was Discerning of His Students

I realize at this point that Jesus, again, had an advantage over us. He possessed intuitive knowledge. We do not. We have to learn things about others. Jesus already knows.

A brief survey as to how Jesus reacted with others reveals that He knew something about the people to whom He ministered. Knowing them determined how He related to them. Note a few examples:

- With Nicodemus He discussed theology,
  John 3:1-10
- With the woman at the well, He talked about water,
  John 4:7-29
- With the Apostle Peter, He scolded him,
  Matthew 26:31-35
- With the widow, He knew how much money she had,
  Luke 21:1-4
- With Thomas, He knew he had some doubts,
  John 20:24-29
- With the adulterous woman, He knew her past,
  John 8:1-11
- With Nathaniel, He knew who he was,
  John 1:46-51

I can tell you by experience that the more you know about your students; the better you will understand them. There have been so many times when I would have problems with students and not know why. Then I would learn something about them, about their parents, about their personal situations, and it was like a light going on in my head. I understood them. Understanding them by knowing something about them made all the difference in the world.

Perhaps you're thinking, "Yeah, that sounds good about Jesus knowing people but He didn't have the kind of students I've had." Let's reverse that statement. You and I may never have had the kind of students He had. How would you have handled Judas? Thomas? Peter? Nicodemus? Jesus had to deal with some of the most repulsive, stubborn, sinful people

They Call Me Doc

you can imagine. The thing that always brings conviction to my own heart is how tender and compassionate Jesus was, with the worse kind of people, and yet how stern He was with religious hypocrisy. I think sometimes we get it all backwards.

He Was Dedicated To the Scriptures

More than ever before, I am deeply convinced that one of the greatest tragedies in many churches today is a lack of knowledge regarding the Bible. It's no excuse to say you don't teach the Bible. It's no excuse to say that only people in the "ministry" should know the Bible. The Bible was written for all believers. One of my former colleagues, Dr. Robert Picirilli, used to teach about the ministry with a little "m" and the ministry with a capital "M." Ministry with a capital "M" refers to those in the full-time ministry, or those who make their income in the ministry, such as a full-time pastor or missionary. Ministry with a lower case "m" refers to all believers, regardless of their choice of career. Dr. Picirilli's point was that all Christians, regardless of their status in life and choice of career, have an obligation to serve the Lord. That includes having a working knowledge of the Bible.

Again, Jesus had the advantage over us. He helped in the writing of the Scriptures, but have you ever noticed often in the Lord's earthly ministry how He referred to the Scriptures? When those critics would challenge Him He would say something like, "What did Moses say," or, "Have you never read?"

Do you remember when He was tempted in the wilderness by Satan? Read it in Matthew 4:1-11. In every instance, when Satan tempted Him, Jesus would reply, *"It is written"* (Matthew 4:4, 7, 10). He knew the Scriptures well. If in His body of flesh He had to resort to the Scriptures, how much more do we?

Every Christian should be a student of the Word of God. There's no excuse for teachers to be ignorant of the Bible. I was privileged to attend and graduate from a good Bible college, and believe me when I tell you; it helped to prepare me for the secular world when I enrolled as a graduate student in public institutions. You may not have had the opportunity to attend a Bible college, but in this day of technology you can learn the Bible. There are many resources available but you have to avail yourself of them. If you want to be a teacher like Christ, be dedicated to the Scriptures.

He Was Diverse in His Situations

His diversity is seen in three areas: His classroom, His content, and His conduct.

In His Classroom

Where did Jesus teach? That's an easy question. He taught wherever He happened to be. He didn't need a particular place. Read through the Gospel of John for a quick survey.

His "classroom" consisted of:

- sitting on the side of a well
- sitting in a boat
- speaking in a synagogue

- speaking in the Temple
- speaking from a mountainside
- being in the privacy of someone's home
- being in an enclosed room
- being in the open air
- speaking at night
- speaking in the day time
- and a whole lot more.

Get the picture? Wherever He was and wherever people were became His classroom. He was not confined to one setting. The world was His room. My point for teachers today is that sometimes you'd be better off to move your classroom to a different location, or at least rearrange the one you have. Do something different.

In His Content

I've alluded to this in an earlier chapter, but it bears repeating. His content in many ways depended upon His audience. His teaching depended on what He knew about His students. You may recall that there were those who said that Jesus never spoke like any other person; when they said that, they were usually referring to His knowledge and intellect. On the other hand, no one has ever spoken so simply and clearly as Jesus. As you read through your Bible note how many times He used the simple things of life to teach a spiritual truth. Things like:

- the wind
- flowers
- birds

They Call Me Doc

- water
- seed
- waves
- fish
- bread

Look at that list. Everything on it is simple. We still have every one of them with us today, and they can still be used to teach spiritual truths. I once overhead a group of students talking about two teachers. They said that one made simple things hard, the other made hard things simple. Which one are you? Don't get me wrong, there are times when teachers have to deal with difficult topics. But I have had difficult classes where the teacher made things understandable, and I've had other classes where I thought the teacher was trying to impress me with his knowledge. Both of them succeeded.

In His Conduct

By conduct, I'm referring to the methods Jesus used. He was diverse in His approach to both the subject at hand and the students involved. Look at the list regarding how simply Jesus taught and you will get a glimpse of some of His methods, such as:

- Visuals
- One on one
- Small groups
- Large groups
- Discussion
- Questions and answers
- Hypothetical situations
- Thought provoking

They Call Me Doc

Several years ago the Administration of Free Will Baptist Bible College sponsored a series of seminars for the faculty and student body by a Christian organization known as Faith Visuals. The main speaker was a very talented lady who was most proficient with an overhead projector. This was in the days when power-point presentations had not yet been heard of. She was absolutely amazing with her ability, even creating "motion" with a still machine. I remember that in one of her presentations, she made this statement: "If Jesus were on earth today, He would use an overhead projector." That may have been a tongue-in-cheek comment, but her point was, Jesus used whatever methods were available to Him at the time. My son, Kevin, who is also a college professor tells me he believes that if Jesus were alive today He would probably use a power point for his presentation.

Obviously, we have far more technology than Jesus had, but I don't want you to miss an important point. The point is this: even without technology, you are a visual. You have a voice that can be lower or louder. You have a body that can be utilized as a means of demonstrating your point. You have the ability to smile, or frown. You are a visual aid.

I recall hearing about a teacher of history who always kept his students in suspense, because they never knew what he would look like when he came to class. Whatever historical period of time he was teaching; he would come dressed in the clothing of that era. He made quite an impact on his students. I've done some of that myself on a smaller scale. When I taught the Gospel of John at Free Will Baptist College and described what the Jews were like, I would arrange to take my class to the Jewish synagogue, located

They Call Me Doc

nearby, to hear the Rabbi speak. He was always more than gracious to answer their questions.

When we would get to the resurrection of Jesus, occasionally I would take the class to a local cemetery that had an exact replica of the tomb of Jesus on display. At other times I would allow the students to act out a scene. The one I recall best was the day the class went to the gymnasium swimming pool to see one of the students portray John the Baptist baptizing another student who portrayed Jesus. I still get comments about these "field trips."

Jesus was the ultimate educator because He demonstrated what He said, He desired to serve, He was discerning of His students, He was dedicated to the Scriptures, and He was diverse in His situations. What a model we have to follow!

They Call Me Doc

Effective Bible Teaching*

"You all pray for me today. I didn't know I was supposed to teach. Brother Stanley, you read the first verse and tell us what it means." Brother Stanley reads the verse and remarks, "It means what it says." This particular scene has been duplicated too many times in too many church settings. It's ironic that people who say they believe the Bible often times treat it so haphazardly when it comes to teaching it. If we believe the Bible like we say we do, why is so much of our teaching of the Bible so bland and ineffective?

There are two key ingredients in teaching, regardless of the subject matter. It makes no difference the age level, the curriculum, or the situation, the ingredients are the same. Whether the material is based on Scripture or something that is considered to be secular doesn't change the fact. The two ingredients in any, and every, teaching opportunity are preparation and presentation.

PREPARATION

In all areas of life preparation is vital. We expect it in areas like medicine and law. None of us would knowingly go to a doctor for surgery if we knew the surgeon was unprepared or ill-prepared. We want to be sure the mechanic who services our vehicles knows what he is doing. If we need a lawyer we want one who knows the law. In the field of education we expect those who teach our children to be trained in educational procedures. We want the best teachers we can get. We want them to be qualified, certified, and have the proper license. And rightly we should. But why is it, when it comes to teaching the Bible we somehow take a different approach? Why it is that Sunday school teachers are not required to meet some kind of standard before they teach? This is not to say that all of those who are teaching in churches today are ineffective, but many are woefully lacking in training, knowledge, and preparation. Neither do I mean to say that all teachers in church need to have Bible college training, but too often they have no preparation at all.

Preparation, while it may involve a formalized approach, is basically personal. It is the time a teacher spends getting ready. At least three areas of preparation should be considered: (1) of yourself; (2) of the content of the lesson; and (3) of the classroom.

Preparation of Yourself

Every aspect of yourself is involved in teaching. This is true regardless of the level you teach. Teaching involves physical, emotional, social, intellectual, and spiritual preparation. Each of these areas must be prepared if teaching is to be effective. The amount of rest you get on Saturday night will make a difference in your effectiveness on Sunday morning. How you relate to others in your classroom may very well hinge on how you feel physically. What you have personally learned, or haven't learned, as you studied the lesson will be obvious. I remember one of my Bible teachers from college saying it like this: "Don't tell people you're not prepared to teach. They'll know it." The type of preparation that is needed to be effective cannot be accomplished in a few minutes; it's a process that becomes a part of your personality.

Several years ago I had the privilege of hearing a very

They Call Me Doc

well-known preacher and expositor of the Scripture. He has written many commentaries and is considered to be very fundamental. He is a good communicator of truth. After one of his speaking sessions, the audience was invited to another room to have a personal time of questions and answers with him. I took the opportunity. I will never forget one of the questions and the answer he gave. He was asked, "How do you get so much out of just one verse or phrase of the Bible?" His answer both shocked and convicted me. He responded, "It has nothing to do with brain power. It has to do with staying still long enough until I'm sure I understand what is being said. If I don't understand it, I keep digging until I do. I refuse to teach something without knowing what it means." I left with the determination to be that kind of teacher.

I believe that preparation of yourself involves getting ready the night before. It may seem trivial, and maybe even ridiculous, but knowing before you go to bed what you're going to wear the next morning cuts down on a lot of frustration. Not finding what you want to wear can put your mind in a different gear and cause your attitude to be on edge. Having to look for socks or iron a shirt at the last minute may not appear to be spiritual, but believe me, your spiritual attitude can be determined by such little things.

Preparation of the Content of the Lesson

Studying a particular passage, or lesson, involves your preference and habits of learning. There are some good methods of Bible study but no method is better than your personal desire and attitude. You should want to prepare; you should want to give a good presentation. This kind of

They Call Me Doc

preparation takes time. It is an ongoing activity instead of a last minute affair. It begins long before the Saturday night before the lesson is to be taught. Reading the lesson well in advance gives your mind the opportunity to meditate and think. As you prepare yourself to know the content of the lesson, your mind will begin to think of some ways, or methods, to best teach that truth. Understanding the background of a passage makes it clearer to you and consequently makes it more enjoyable for your students.

Preparation of the Classroom

I realize your classroom may already be determined. In some cases, you may not have a choice. You may be forced to be in a small room with poor lighting but there are still some things you can do. Ask yourself these questions: What does the room look like? Is it colorful or drab? Is it dirty or clean? Could the lighting be changed without a lot of expense? Are the chairs appropriate to the age of the students? Would tables be better? Would it be convenient to rearrange the chairs if necessary? Every teacher in public and private schools has a planning period where these kinds of questions are dealt with. Your planning period may need to be at home, but don't wait until the day of the lesson to begin that planning.

PRESENTATION

This aspect of teaching is where the rubber meets the road. All the preparation now becomes presentation. Your presentation is an overflow of your preparation. Poor preparation produces poor presentation. In other words, good preparation makes for a good presentation.

They Call Me Doc

Presentation involves methods, materials, the use of your voice, and enthusiasm. It is your preparation on display.

The day is long gone when you can stand in front of your class with the teacher's manual in your hand or have someone read from their printed material. The Bible deserves far more than that. Let me give a few suggestions.

Be Enthusiastic

Enthusiasm is contagious. I'm not talking about something fake, but something genuine. When the teacher is excited about the class, the students sense that. Enthusiasm is based on what you have personally gleaned from your preparation. Enthusiasm implies you enjoy what you're doing.

Do Something Different

Instead of using the same method over and over, do something different. Rearrange the room. Make use of appropriate visuals, or other forms of media. Have a discussion. Involve members of the class with the teaching. Don't be the only one who talks.

Expect Something from the Class

"Wait a minute. I have a hard enough time just getting them to come to class. How can I make any expectations for them?" Is it possible that the reason some of them do not come is that nothing is expected of them? Nothing motivates learning like learning something you didn't know before. Take for instance something like asking a question. When you ask a question, expect someone to answer. Don't answer

They Call Me Doc

for them. Learn to "wait them out." The silence will soon become boring and before long someone will break the silence and say something. It's simply a fact of life: people do what is expected of them, but when no expectations are required, they do nothing. Ask a question that requires more than just a "yes" or "no" response. Ask something that requires more than just an agreement with you. Don't be afraid to have disagreements. Obviously, you want to be civil and polite, but differences of opinion can be beneficial.

Let me mention something about having questions or doubts about something the Bible says. Is it wrong to doubt the Bible? Just because you don't know what something means doesn't mean you doubt the Bible. Quite often when I'm reading my Bible and read something that I don't fully understand, I will literally take a pen or highlighter and put a question mark in the margin of my Bible. That question motivates me to find the answer, such as:

1. When God told Elijah to pour water on the sacrifice, where did Elijah get the water? It hadn't rained in almost three years.

2. When Jesus cursed the fig tree it withered and died, but one of the Bible writers says it wasn't time for the figs. Why did Jesus curse a tree for not having figs when it wasn't time to have figs?

3. When God became angry with Moses and wanted to kill him, what was God angry about? Why did He want to kill Moses?

They Call Me Doc

    4. Was Judas a Christian? If he wasn't, why did the Lord allow him to be in His band of disciples?

When I find the answers to these questions, which I have, I get thrilled about removing the question mark from the margin, but the point is, the question does not mean disbelief. It drives me to find out, and when I discover the answer my faith is always strengthened, never weakened. Jesus was a Master Teacher, and as such He knew the importance of an effective presentation. Study His life carefully. Granted, He was God in the flesh, but He always practiced good educational principles in His teaching. His presentation included being aware of His audience or students. He met them on their level and challenged them to rise higher. He challenged them to think. He expected something from them. He used the methods that were common in His day. The glorious thought for us is that we have the opportunity to have His mind in us and to be as effective in our teaching as He was.

---

* This portion, written by Ken Riggs, has been reprinted with permission from Randall House Publications, National Association of Free Will Baptists, from a previous publication.

They Call Me Doc

Teaching Attributes Personified

One of the most recent books to hit the market regarding what constitutes good teachers is *What Great Teachers Do Differently: 14 Things That Matter Most*, authored by Todd Whitaker. It's a book that school districts and administrators are trying to get teachers to read. I have read it. It's well written, easy to read, and thought provoking. I even use parts of it in my Educational Psychology classes for Nashville State Community College. Just in case those of you reading this do not have a chance to read what Whitaker says, let me summarize, in my words, what I think his research revealed. I am merely listing them without comment for you to compare his list with mine.

- People are more important than programs
- Be willing to expect students to do something
- Stop some bad behavior before it ever begins
- High expectations should be for everyone, including the teacher
- Teachers are the variables in the classroom and they should always improve
- A positive attitude, environment, and praise go a long way
- Take what you hear from students and teachers with a grain of salt
- Admit when something you've done didn't work or was just plain wrong
- Be willing to be flexible and adjust when necessary
- Challenge slower students to rise higher
- Challenge all students to rise higher
- Treat everyone as being good, even if they're not

They Call Me Doc

- Keep standardized testing in its proper perspective
- Students don't care what you know until they know that you care

While I do not even come close to the expertise of Mr. Whitaker, I want to offer what I have observed constitutes good teaching. My list is based on personal contact with teachers in a classroom setting. In a few cases they crossed my path in other ways but still taught me something. Truthfully, each of them could easily be listed for more than one characteristic, but one is all I will mention. While the characteristic is important, of greater importance is the character of the individual. I am not revealing the names of any individual, but I will state the area where their characteristic was prominent.

Administrative Skills

Every teacher has to have administrative skills. In one sense every teacher is the administrator of their subject matter and classroom. It's not my purpose here to give a lengthy discussion of what an administrator does. My purpose is to mention the individual in my teaching career who possessed this essential characteristic.

I was fortunate to have had three administrators who were most efficient. One was a college president, one was a pastor, and one was a director of a Christian education agency. The college president I had known for a long time. He and my father were good friends. His oldest son and I went to rival high schools and played basketball against each other. When I joined the college faculty under this administrator, I soon learned about another younger son who

They Call Me Doc

eventually became a colleague and friend.

The administrative skills of this college president were many. It was not just his skills that impressed me. It was his appearance. I'm not sure what a college president is to look like, but he looked like one. His appearance was always flawless. He looked "presidential"; he acted like a president. I had the privilege of having him as a teacher for one class. My main relationship to him was as a member of the faculty. It was obvious to everyone who was in charge. He had a competent staff of others around him, but I always knew he was in charge, but he was not arrogant about it. We had several conversations through the years I was there, and even for a time I served as his pastor. But here's the thing that impressed me. When I was hired to be on the faculty and have the privilege of working under his supervision, he called me into his office. At first I was a little intimidated because his very aura was impressive. He soon put me at ease. He said, "Kenneth (he was the only one on campus who called me that), I really hope your experience here works out. I want to make you a promise. If the program succeeds, you'll get the credit. If it fails, I'll take the blame."

Wow! How can you lose with that kind of support? I wanted to do well but more importantly, he wanted me to do well. He knew what it meant to give people the opportunity to do their job. He knew how to delegate, or at least that's what I felt. Too many administrators hire people but then cramp their style, but not this man. I'm sure if I had done something out of line, he would have reprimanded me, but my relationship with him was always a good one.

While the other two administrators with whom I

They Call Me Doc

worked, did not say the exact same thing as the college president, they knew the importance of the concept of delegation. They told me my job but gave me the liberty to do it in the way I felt it should be done. These three men reminded me of a principle in working with people that I have strived to live by: It's amazing how much can be accomplished if you don't care who gets the credit. I've revised that slightly by saying; it's amazing what can be accomplished if you give the Lord the credit. These three men did that.

Faith in God and Faith in Others

Students know whether you like them or not. My personal theory is that when students are afraid of you, you don't teach them very much. That doesn't mean teachers should be "buddy buddy" and a "pal," but it does mean that students need to feel appreciated. The teacher who personified this to me was a teacher in one of my graduate courses. He was a rather large man who lectured as he sat cross-legged on the desk. He had no notes or visual aids. He just talked. I'm not sure why or how we hit it off, but we did. It might have been because he was not afraid to tell of his faith. The class only met on Saturday mornings. Typically, he would announce a week in advance what his lecture would be the following week. One particular Saturday he announced that the next week he would be lecturing on the subject, "Why I am a Christian and why I believe the Bible to be the Word of God." This was a secular college. I could hardly wait until the next week. Usually several people were absent, but on this day, almost everyone attended. He began his lecture by stating, "I'm speaking on this subject because if I don't, some of you will never hear the truth about Christ and the Bible." I told him after class how much I appreciated his comments and how it had encouraged me not to be ashamed of my faith outside of the "religious arena." He expressed an appreciation for me that has stayed with me until this day.

Commitment

Teachers who stay with it for several years do so because they enjoy what they're doing. It usually is not because of money. Because of my family background, I had known of this individual for quite some time even before I actually met him. It was not until I became a student at Free Will Baptist Bible College that I began to know him better. I had him as a teacher in Bible and Christian Education classes and he was committed to both, but to me, where he excelled was in the pulpit as a preacher. He was committed to the Bible and nothing would deter him from that. In fact, on one occasion when a special speaker spoke for a service, the speaker said something that was contrary to the doctrinal belief of the Free Will Baptist denomination. When the speaker finished, this individual, before dismissing the service, politely, but forcefully made a public comment showing his displeasure with what the speaker had said.

It was this individual who encouraged me to become a teacher, who stayed in contact with me about joining the college faculty. At Christmas of 1990, he and his wife presented members of the faculty a copy of the *One Year Bible*. I have faithfully read it through each year since that time and have committed myself to read it, believe it, and teach it. Another comment of his when I was a student has proven to be true as well. He would say, "Be ready to preach, pray, or

They Call Me Doc

die at a minute's notice." I've learned that is true as well. Now as a preacher, I carry a list of outlines I have preached just in case I get an unannounced or on-the-spot opportunity to preach.

Courage

You may not think teachers need courage but believe me they do. They need courage as believers not to be afraid to stand for truth in a dark, unsaved world. They need courage to stand for what they think is right even against fellow Christians. In fact, that may be the greater challenge. Such is the case of a couple with whom I have worked. When Carolyn and I married, this couple was employed by what was then the Free Will Baptist League, later to become the Church Training Service Department. I was hired to work with them. My job was to fill orders and see that they were properly mailed to churches. We worked in a run-down garage and a little nicer building that had been a home that doubled as office space for the National Association of Free Will Baptists.

I don't remember the exact date but the husband was promoted to be the Director. The denomination was going through some changes to curriculum for both League and Sunday school. Competitive activities for young people were being introduced to the denomination, and later on a concept of Christian camping was introduced. At the time, the League Board owned property in White Bluff, Tennessee, about 30 miles west of Nashville. I worked with this couple my junior and senior years as a student at Free Will Baptist Bible College. After graduation, I continued to work, but now some of my responsibilities included traveling as a Youth

They Call Me Doc

Evangelist. I heard the criticism that was hurled at them for wanting to make changes in curriculum. I heard the criticism they received because they did not have the lifestyle, or convictions about things that others might have had. But never one time did I ever hear them complain or show an attitude of revenge. They just kept on doing their ministry.

Issues forced the denomination to inform the Church Training Service Department to change their financial status. The camp concept, known as Hillmont, was costing too much money so it had to be sold. Business arrangements were made, the property was sold, and this couple bought the property and were able to continue in what they believed was God's will for their lives. Being wise stewards, they legally incorporated and the camp is now governed by a Board of Directors. The Hillmont Camp is a thriving retreat and conference center for numerous churches and individuals around the Nashville area as well as surrounding states. Their courage has inspired me to stand for what I think is right and feel called of God to do.

Excellence

She used to be known as the First Lady of Free Will Baptist Bible College when her husband was President. She was a speech teacher. I had her for my speech classes. Quite frankly, I didn't want to take speech because at the time I didn't think I would ever be speaking in front of an audience. I had a terrible lisp and I didn't see any good reason for taking a speech class. I had already been through speech therapy in elementary school, and I sure didn't want to go through that again.

They Call Me Doc

If you know her, you know she is proficient in diction and communication. I can still see her in my mind's eye as she did one of her monologues in class as well as in a vesper service. The two that stand out to me are the ones about the young lady who goes through the various stages of life from being a young maiden, wife, mother, and elderly lady. The other one is about a married couple who lives in poverty and cannot afford even the necessities of life, yet their love for each other causes them to sacrifice for each other.

One of her speech assignments was for us to develop a "Poetry Program." You were to gather a series of poems with a related theme, memorize every one of them, and recite the program in front of the class. It had to be done with the proper pronunciation of the words, the feeling of the poet, and bodily expression. The best ones would be chosen to give their programs in a chapel service. As you developed your program, she would check with you to see how you were coming. She would be careful, but tactful, to point out what you could do better. All I wanted to do was memorize it and get it over with. I chose to develop poetry around the theme of the cross. When I gave my program in front of the class I was relieved. That would be the last time for that. After class she informed me I was to give my program in chapel the next week! That experience bolstered my confidence: that even with my lisp I could speak in public, if I would strive to do a good job. I've been speaking in public now for a long time. She displayed an attitude of excellence in herself and expected no less from all of us.

Friendship

Having a teacher that becomes a lifelong friend is not only

rare, it's a blessing. Earlier, I made a comment that a teacher should not become a pal, particularly to the point that you lose your responsibility to be a teacher. Even so, being a friend to students can change their lives. Such is the case I have enjoyed with a music teacher. He was my voice instructor and taught me how to use my diaphragm, how to direct a congregation, and how to be a friend. While he became a friend, he did not show favoritism. If you were to sing at a local church as a guest soloist or member of a choir or quartet, he would meet you on Sunday morning to be sure you had everything right. He would not accept sloppy performances.

A friend is someone with whom you can have a good laugh. I've had my share with him. On one occasion I was singing in a quartet with some friends of mine, one of whom had just recently gotten false teeth. I don't recall what occurred but in the course of rehearsal, something was said from the student with his new teeth that struck the teacher's fancy and he responded, "Truer words never came from falser teeth." Only a friend could say that. Another time in a rehearsal, he reminded us that if someone says to you, "You sing warmly, just remember that's not so hot."

Long after he moved to another teaching position, we have maintained a friendship. Not too many years ago, it was a blessing to have him and his wife return to Nashville for a choir reunion with former members of the choirs he had directed at Free Will Baptist Bible College, and with former faculty members and staff with whom he had worked. Through the technology of e-mail, we correspond periodically even today.

They Call Me Doc

Loyalty

A classroom teacher needs to feel the loyalty of those over him. Teachers need to believe that principals are behind them. Teachers need to know they can count on those over them when they are confronted with irate parents or unruly students or dozens of other issues. Most of my teaching career has been at the college level, and I was fortunate to sense that kind of loyalty from a college dean who displayed that characteristic to me. It was not just a sense of loyalty that I felt for my teaching. It was a sense of loyalty in several areas. For a time we even worked together in a local church. Even while I was still a student he was serving as pastor and I was the music director. After joining the faculty, there was that loyalty to my teaching. Don't misunderstand: he and I had some conversations that revealed some disagreements, such as my feelings about a Liberal Arts approach to accreditation instead of accreditation by the American Association of Bible Colleges, and why girls had to major in Bible since no church would hire a girl as a pastor. He told me that I was not very realistic about some of my views, but I still felt his loyalty.

I do remember when the denomination was involved in some touchy issues that directly involved the college and my teaching area in particular; I always knew I had his support. There was a time when there were those outside the college faculty and staff who wanted me to leave my position because I didn't agree with some of their issues. I went to him and talked with him about it. After that, when those who wanted me to leave approached me about it, I would say to them, "Until either the Lord or my dean tells me to leave, I'm staying here."

They Call Me Doc

He was one of four faculty members who consistently mingled with the students, particularly on the basketball court. Frequently, the four of us would meet in the gym to play some "pick-up" ballgames with students and then play in an annual Faculty-Senior ballgame. I sang with him in a quartet as well.

When our oldest son was born, Carolyn and I lived close to him and his family. We lived in an attic apartment with no air-conditioning and our son was born in July. This man and his family had to be away for a length of time and graciously offered their home to us while they were away so that my wife and I and our new son would be more comfortable. On another occasion the two of us traveled to Albany, Georgia, to conduct a week-end Bible Conference. I've never known a more loyal Free Will Baptist, preacher, scholar, and friend like him. His loyalty is to be commended and I have greatly appreciated his loyalty to me.

Love

You would expect a teacher to have the characteristic of love regardless of the age level, the topic, or the curriculum. But love is one of those words that is often difficult to define. It's probably better demonstrated than defined. In one sense, all the characteristics and people I have suggested possessed love. That is, in actuality everything we do that is good, proper, and wholesome stems from love. But there are some people who display love better than others. The individual who characterized the attribute of love was a former denominational executive leader and pastor. Because of the relationship I had with this individual, I will reveal his name. It was my father, Rev. Raymond Riggs. When he asked me to

They Call Me Doc

be the Principal of the Bethany Christian School in Norfolk, Virginia, I went because I sensed it was the right thing to do. However, I had another motive. I had watched him through the years, not as a son watching a father, but as a fellow minister watching another minister. My dad has always been respected among his peers and I wanted to know why. What was it about him that was different? A dear friend of mine told me one time, "If I ever backslide, I want Raymond Riggs to give the invitation because I know I'll return to the Lord."

Daddy had a genuine love for people. That was his secret. That's why people were attracted to him. I've seen him in a church business meeting calm the situation just by saying a few words. I've seen him on the floor of the National Association of Free Will Baptists, during heated discussions, sway the audience. I've seen him deal with all classes of people and it made no difference to him who you were. He loved you and somehow you knew it. That characteristic is what every teacher should possess. Don't get me wrong, he was stern. His love was not the kind that made him a pushover. He knew how to stand his ground but he did it with a loving attitude. Long before the term "tough love" was introduced into our vocabulary, Daddy was displaying it. Students need their teachers to be firm, but they need firmness that is cradled in love.

Compilation of Attributes

If you've been keeping up with this section of attributes and characteristics, you have probably noticed that it's a rather lengthy list. It totals twenty-seven in all. As a reminder, read them again.

They Call Me Doc

Jesus Christ
1. He demonstrated what He said
2. He desired to serve
3. He was discerning of His students
4. He was dedicated to the Scriptures
5. He was diverse in His situations

What Great Teachers Do Differently
(Todd Whitaker)
1. People are more important than programs
2. Be willing to expect something from students
3. Stop bad behavior before it starts
4. High expectations should be required for everyone
5. Be aware of variables in education
6. Sincere and honest praise is powerful
7. Take what you hear with a grain of salt
8. Admit when something doesn't work or is wrong
9. Ignore some things
10. Challenge slower students to rise higher
11. Challenge all students to higher levels
12. Treat everyone as good, even if they're not
13. Students don't care what you know until they know that you care
14. Watch out for standardized tests

Attributes personified
1. Administrative skills
2. Faith in God and faith in others
3. Commitment
4. Courage
5. Excellence
6. Friendship
7. Loyalty
8. Love

They Call Me Doc

Quite frankly, that's a tall order for any teacher. You could probably find many more attributes by making your own list. No doubt just a casual visit to a local bookstore, browsing what's available would give you even more. Here's the point of this: what makes a good teacher often depends upon your experience with a particular teacher. What is a good teacher to some may not be to others, but the challenge is great. Every teacher should constantly be striving to be the absolute best.

I want to mention one more thing about the characteristics of a good teacher. For several years I've made it a practice to ask two questions of my students who are planning to be teachers. The questions are these: (1) Why do you want to be a teacher, and (2) What do you remember about teachers you've had in the past? The answers to both of these are quite revealing.

The responses I have heard the most frequently to the first question are:

1. I like learning and want to teach others
2. I remember a teacher who had a big influence in my life
3. I want to help someone like a teacher who helped me

The responses to the second question are equally revealing:

1. They were very patient with me
2. They made things easy to understand
3. They took a personal interest in me
4. They acted like they really cared about me

They Call Me Doc

I find their answers interesting because most of the time it's not where the teachers may have gone to college, or what kind of degree they attained. It's not necessarily how much knowledge a teacher may have or what honors he may have received. Please don't misunderstand that. I believe teachers should be trained, qualified, and have proper credentials, but I sometimes wonder if those things don't become more important to others than they do to the actual students in the classrooms. Most students may not remember much about the subject matter they were taught, but they definitely remember what they liked and didn't like about the teacher.

Section Three

It Happened in the Classroom

They Call Me Doc

It Happened in the Classroom

As a teacher, one thing is for sure: the day is never boring. You never know what's going to happen. When I began writing this book, I debated as to what to call this section. I started to call it "You've Got to Be Kidding", or "You'll Never Believe This." The truth is, I'm not kidding and you may not believe some of the experiences I've had. In telling some of the antics that have occurred, I will not divulge the names of any individuals, and for those reading this who may have been involved with these antics, I hope you're grateful. The antics happened in a variety of places such as elementary, middle, high school, college, and some in Sunday school or other church related activities. Since I'm a minister as well as a teacher, I've even included some that have happened at funerals and weddings. In most cases, it will be obvious but if it's not, use your imagine. The order in writing these has no significance whatsoever. Some are humorous; some are less humorous, but all are true.

What's Behind the Door?

If you've ever conducted a chapel service for elementary children, you might identify with this one, or something similar. Get the picture in your mind. A speaker is telling a Bible story. It's a story that explains on a child's level the truth of the gospel. At the conclusion of the story, the speaker has the children close their eyes and bow their heads. Children are invited to come forward if they want to talk farther about the gospel. Behind the speaker is a folding accordion door that separates the room into two parts. As some of the children come forward, they are ushered behind

They Call Me Doc

the accordion door for privacy. However, after a few children have already gone behind the door, one more child came forward. Wanting to be helpful, the speaker quietly says to the child, "Why did you come forward?" to which the child answered, "I want to see what's behind the door." The speaker wisely let the child go and see.

The Light is Off!

Many Christian schools utilize a church building that is also used for Sunday school rooms on Sunday. Often time events are planned at the church to encourage those students who may attend the school, but do not attend a church to come to a special program. When children are at school during the week, they are taught when they go to the restroom to leave the light on. If the light is off when a child goes to the restroom, they are asked to go get their teacher. On one occasion one student whose family did not attend church at all, visited a church service. The little boy needed to go to the restroom, so he quietly got up from his seat in the auditorium and walked to where he knew the restrooms were. As luck, or whatever, would have it, the light in the restroom was off. The little boy marched back into the auditorium and went to the front row where I was seated and loudly announced, "The light is off in the bathroom." The speaker had no choice but to stop and let everyone savor the moment.

Brief Articles

As a college teacher, one of my standing assignments for my classes was to have students keep up with local news and current events. To hold them accountable, I asked them to

They Call Me Doc

write a brief summary of what they had read and be prepared to turn their summaries in at the end of the semester. On the day the summaries were to be turned in, one student approached me before class began to tell me his articles were in the process of being copied and someone would bring them before the end of class. I continued with the class. Just before the final bell, there was a knock on the door. I went to the door and there stood another young man with an envelope and told me the brief summaries were in the envelope. I thanked him, but as soon as I took the envelope and felt of it, I knew I had been had. The "brief" articles were written on briefs! No, I didn't show them to the class. Fortunately, the briefs were clean.

Identical Term Papers

When grading term papers, teachers have learned that it's a good practice to read a paper without knowing whose paper is being graded until the grade has been assigned. I was reading a stack of papers and after reading a very good paper, I assigned the grade of "A", laid the paper on a stack and continued to read others. A few papers later, I was reading and realized I had already read this paper and assumed I must have picked it up off the wrong stack. When I checked, the paper I had already graded was in the stack where I had placed it, but the paper I was reading was identical. The only difference in the two papers was the names of the two individuals. I was stunned. I knew I would have to deal with it, so I notified the two students to come to my office. As they entered my office I asked them if they knew why I had called them. They had no idea. When I showed them the identical papers, they were floored. Neither one had honestly known what had happened. After a little more discussion, I

They Call Me Doc

learned the situation. Both of them had another class together with another teacher. That teacher, to be of help, had passed out a model term paper. Instead of each of these two individuals writing their own papers, they had merely put their names on the model the teacher had given to them and turned it into me. I quoted a verse to them that my father had quoted to me as a matter of principle when I was growing up. The verse was *"...be sure your sins will find you out"* (Numbers 32:23). I gave them both an F for the paper.

Hide Under a Chicken

In teaching Christian Education of Children, one of the assignments was to tell a Bible story on the age level of your choice to the entire class. Before telling the story you had selected, you were to explain the purpose of your story and what age you thought the story was appropriate for. The class would then, within reason, role play the age of the children involved. One young man chose to tell the story of the mother hen protecting her brood of chicks. As the story went, the hen house caught fire and the mother hen gathered her chicks under her wings to save them, but in the process she was killed. To make the application, the student began to explain that as the mother hen was willing to give her life for her chicks, Jesus was willing to die for us. As the student concluded, he asked the class to explain the meaning of the story. One of his peers said, "When your house catches on fire, hide under a chicken." It was another one of the laughing moments.

Pfft! And He Was Gone

An interesting time in any class is when you have students

They Call Me Doc

who are not native to America and American cultures. Such was the case of a young black man from Nigeria. It was in the Gospel of John. The young man always sat up front because he wanted to be sure he could understand what was being said. Things went very well, and he was a good student. However, the day I was to explain the resurrection of Jesus Christ is a day I will not soon forget. I was trying to explain the process of the Lord's body being lifted up from the grave and yet the grave clothes were left in the tomb. Jesus had simply disappeared and left the grave clothes behind. I knew it was an instantaneous event, so in trying to capture that spirit I said, "PFFT! His body was gone." When I looked at the young man I couldn't help but notice how white his eye balls appeared against his very black skin. He looked at me with astonishment and asked, "Professor Riggs, how do you spell pffft?" I wasn't sure but I said, " P-F-F-F-T." It was another good laugh, not at him, but with him.

Hiding under a Bush

This has nothing to do with the children's chorus that talks about hiding a candle under a bushel. It was a night class in the book of James. I'll be the first to admit that after classes all day, it's hard for some students to be motivated to come to a night class. The same is true of teachers. This particular night, I noticed that two young men, who were normally there, were absent. I thought nothing about it and went on with the class. When class was over, I made my way to the back parking lot behind the classroom to get in my car to go home. As I walked out in the parking lot, I saw one of the absent young men in the parking lot. Out of the corner of my left eye, I saw the other one but he was running to hide under a bush next to the building. I made no mention of

They Call Me Doc

him, but I said to the other young man. "Missed you in class tonight, and tell your friend I saw him trying to hide under the bush." It's very hard to hide under a small bush when you're six feet, nine inches tall. When I see them, we still laugh about it.

Tell Mrs. Nelson You Were Kidding

This was in a Sunday school session. The class met in the church auditorium. A student from one of my Christian Education classes was the teacher. It was time for class to begin, but the teacher had not arrived. I had taught my classes to not only be on time, but to be a few minutes early, but he was neither. Behind me sat another student whom I knew, so I asked him where Sam (not his real name) was. He didn't know either. A few more minutes went by and finally Sam arrived. He went to the front of the class and said something like, "I don't want to teach this class anymore. Get Riggs to teach." Then he sat down on the front row. I was really getting frustrated now because he had brought me into the situation. I noticed one of the older ladies seemed to almost be in tears about what was happening. As I bowed my head in embarrassment, the student behind me tapped me on the shoulder and motioned for me to look at Sam. He was now standing behind the podium with a smile on his face. He stood in a silence for just a few moments and then said, "Do I have your attention now?" He then proceeded to teach from Jeremiah 20:9 where Jeremiah says there was a time in his life when he felt like giving up and was not going to preach any more, but he couldn't quit. After class, I told him I was proud of him. He said, "Well, you told us to try something different." I then asked him to go and speak to the older lady and tell her he was just kidding about being

They Call Me Doc

aggravated.

Reverse Psychology Gone Bad

Our culture today doesn't look upon paddling in school like it did years ago. In my time, if you received a paddling at school, you got one when you got home because you had gotten one in school. In my earlier days as a principal, I occasionally had to paddle a student, but I never liked it. "Occasionally" is not the right word for two elementary boys that were constantly being sent to me by the teacher. They didn't just "occasionally" come to me; they "often" came to me. Often describes them better. I had paddled them so often that I was getting tired of it. It just didn't seem to be working. As it was bound to happen, they were sent to me again. I talked with them, even pleaded with them to straighten up. Then I had an idea. "Fellows, I want you to know, it doesn't feel good to have to paddle you. To let you know what I mean, I'm going to let you paddle me." Their eyes got real big. I handed them a paddle, bent over the desk, and told each of them to paddle me three times. They did and it stung all six times. It was soon the talk of the school that the principal had been paddled. I never did that again!

Welcome to Sociology

It was well known on the campus of Free Will Baptist Bible College that Joe Jones and I were best of friends. We still are. He was the speech and drama teacher but during the summers, he frequently taught sociology. On the first day of summer school one year, Joe came to my office and asked me to do him a favor. He was going to his class but he wanted me to come about ten minutes later and interrupt him. He

They Call Me Doc

wanted me to ad lib and merely make up something so he would have to leave the room. I agreed, and when the time came, I didn't knock on the door; I merely barged in and said, "Mr. Jones, I need to see you right now." Joe said something like, "Well, I can't come right now. I'm in class." I said something like, "I don't care. I don't appreciate what you've done, and I want to see you in the hall right now." I left the room in a huff and Joe followed close behind. We looked in the small window in the door and the students were in a state of shock. Joe opened the door and we both walked in with a smile on our faces. Then Joe said, "Welcome to Sociology. We're going to learn how to get along with others."

Hiding in the Closet

Mr. Jones and I occupied offices on the third floor of the Academic Building. Quite often we would pull pranks on each other, usually by hiding in a closet and then jumping out to scare each other. One morning as I stood looking out my office window, I noticed Joe pulling into the parking lot. It was now my turn to get him. I went next door to his office and hid in his closet with the idea of waiting until he became preoccupied with something and then I was going to jump out and scare him. I heard his office door open and waited just a few moments and then jumped out. Much to my surprise, however, a student had walked in with him. I scared her more than I did Joe, but all three of us had a good laugh.

You're Not the English Teacher

The one thing about teaching that I dislike the most has to be grading papers. Frequently my classes were required to write a paper, usually on a theme of their choice regarding an

They Call Me Doc

interest they had. I would go over what I expected, how to make an outline, and give them a date for it to be turned in. Papers had been turned in and as I sat reading and grading with red pen in hand, I begin to realize that the paper I was reading was becoming red all over. It had poor grammar, poor sentence structure, and words that didn't come close to being spelled correctly. I put a grade of "F" on the top and had the paper placed in the student's mailbox. The next day the student came to see me and said he wanted to talk about his paper. "Did you even read the content of it?" he asked. "You didn't say anything at all about the topic. You just marked everything red." When I commented that I had read the content but there was so much wrong with it, I couldn't give him a passing grade. To my astonishment he replied as honestly as I've heard anyone, "But you're not the English teacher. I'd understand the red marks if you taught English." He was becoming very irate so I said to him, "I'll tell you what, you take the paper to the dean. If he tells me to change your grade, I'll do it." He left my office but I'm sure he never went to see the dean.

A Concrete Experience

My first full-time position in education was as a teacher of a combined elementary class, principal, bus driver, and music and youth director of the church that sponsored the school. One particular morning while picking up students on a little Volkswagen bus, I stopped to pick up John. He had on a little black mask and a red cape. He was a kindergarten student and today he was dressed like Robin of Batman fame. I opened the door to the bus and said, "Get on the batmobile." When we arrived at school, his teacher rightly told him to take off his costume until recess. At recess time,

They Call Me Doc

he became Robin once again. Not long into recess, I was called to come to the kindergarten area because there had been an accident. As I walked down the hall, I saw him on the floor with a pool of blood circling his head. In the confusion his teacher was telling me what had happened. Next to the door that led out to the playground was a concrete, brick wall. I realized the gash in John's head required stitches so after stopping the blood, I took him to the doctor. On the way I asked John what happened. He was too frightened to talk so I related to him what I was told. "Your teacher tells me that you ran into the brick wall on purpose because you thought you could run through it. Is that what happened?" He responded it was. "Why did you do that?" He responded, "I saw Robin do it." Since that time I have noticed in stores where costumes are sold for children with a warning label that says something like, "CAUTION! Your child might try to fly." In other words, the child may try to assume the identity of the person whose costume he is wearing. I use that story many times in trying to help psychology students understand how literal children are in their thinking.

Hang On to Your False Teeth

Parents are a vital part of the process called education. Sometimes in a positive way, sometimes in a negative way. As an administrator of a school there are many times you are required to meet with parents, unfortunately over something negative that has happened with their child instead of something positive. I've observed most of the discussions revolve around two topics: grades and discipline. On this occasion it was a discussion over a discipline situation. A teacher had disciplined a student but the parent didn't agree

They Call Me Doc

with what had transpired. The parent wanted to see me. Quite often in cases like this, the parents become rather irate. In this case, the parent became irate and animated to the point that her false teeth literally came out of her mouth and she caught them in mid-air. After she caught them, she left the office in embarrassment. I simply laughed, after she was gone, and never heard from her again.

Let Her Get Her Own Beer

One of the things I've tried to teach in my Bible classes is the biblical principle that some things are not what they seem to be. Jesus did several things that were often misunderstood because people failed to recognize that principle. After church one night, my wife asked me to stop at the grocery store to pick up just a couple of items. She stayed in the car and I ran in the store to get what we needed. As I was walking down the aisle, a little short lady said, "Sir, would you get an item off the shelf for me?" I responded I would but when I saw what it was she wanted me to get, I was in a dilemma. Why it wasn't on a lower shelf I don't know, but it was a six pack of beer on the top shelf which she could not reach. I looked around to see if anyone would see me and being convinced no one would, I hastily grabbed a six pack and placed it in her buggy and walked off. The next day in class, I related that story and asked the students what they would have done. Some commended me for helping the lady. One young man, however, in a very serious voice literally said, "Well, bless God, I wouldn't have done it. I would have picked her up and let her get it. I wouldn't have touched the beer." I told him I thought that would have called more attention to what I was doing, but he wasn't convinced.

They Call Me Doc

Duct Tape at a Funeral

Funerals and weddings are my two least favorite things about being a minister, but I've conducted many of both. This particular funeral I will never forget. I had the privilege of being the pastor to a family who lived in the country. When I first met them, very few of them were in church. One son and his wife had been coming on a regular basis. Then the mother and father of the son began coming and I had the privilege of baptizing them. When the mother died, I conducted her funeral. Several years later, the father died and I was asked to conduct the funeral even though I was no longer their pastor. The funeral was in a funeral home and the burial would be in a typical country church cemetery. As we arrived at the church for the burial, the son who had asked me to conduct the funeral informed me his younger brother, who was a grown man, wanted to do something before his father was actually buried. When I asked what he wanted to do, his brother didn't know. After reading Scripture and making a few comments, I then acknowledged the son who wanted to do something. He walked up to the casket with a roll of duct tape and proceeded to put the tape across the top of the casket being sure to put the tape where the casket would be sealed. Then in a rather loud voice he said, "Now you won't get out, you S.O.B!", except he said the actual words and took off running. I never did know what that was about and never asked.

Do You Take This Woman?

This particular wedding was between an older couple who had been married before but each of them had experienced the death of a spouse. They wanted a very small wedding so

They Call Me Doc

it was decided to be in the home of the daughter of the bride. It was going very well until I asked the groom to repeat those familiar vows. I called his name and asked him to repeat after me. After repeating his name, he was to say, "I take thee to be my lawful wedded wife." Instead he said, by accident, "I take thee to be my awful wedded wife."

A Teabag and a Ring

If anything can go wrong, it will go wrong at a wedding. This wedding was a very lovely church wedding for a couple I had known for a long time. Everything was going as rehearsed. It came time for me to ask the groom if he had the ring to give to his bride. He acknowledged that he did and motioned to his best man to give me the ring. This was one of those weddings where the minister was facing the audience as he performed the ceremony. When the best man began to hand me the ring, those sitting close to the front noticed a change in my facial expression. The ring was tied to a Lipton tea bag. It was tied so tightly I couldn't break the string and for a few moments fumbled with it trying to get it untied. Fortunately, the best man had a knife and cut it off for me.

Most of the events I have described that happened in my life were usually when I was either the teacher or the speaker. There are some that occurred when I was a graduate student that I shall never forget.

Experience Your Belly Button

You're reading that right. It definitely says belly button. This happened in a graduate psychology class. The class was

They Call Me Doc

a module class in that it met for an extended period of time on Saturdays only for five weeks but you received a semester's worth of credit. To say the teacher was different is putting it mildly. It was a small class of eleven students. The teacher wanted us to meet at his home but most of the students, including myself, thought that would be an inconvenience. In my case, I was carpooling with some other people and they would have to wait for me to get back to campus after meeting in his home.

There were several oddities about this class but the strangest was the day he announced that we would be learning how to get "in focus with our very being." That should have been my first clue that something weird was about to happen. After explaining how important it is for an individual to understand himself, he asked us to lay our heads on our desks and close our eyes. He then turned the lights out. He began by saying, "Now feel your toes wiggle but don't actually wiggle them. Just experience it's happening without moving them." I honestly tried but had no luck. He then said, "Feel the skin around your shin bone, but don't do it with your hands. Experience the sensation of your shin being touched without touching it." Again, I tried but to no avail.

He continued to tell us to get in touch with our body as he continued naming different parts of the leg, hips, and waist. I still had no luck. Then it happened. He literally said, "Now experience your belly button. Feel the sensation of your finger massaging it but don't actually do it." I lost it and did something I've never done in a class before. I took my hand and slapped my desk very hard and said, "This is ridiculous." With that, he got up from his chair and turned

They Call Me Doc

the lights on.

"Ken I take it you don't approve of this exercise." I tried to remain calm and I did succeed in being polite, but I said, "It has nothing to do with approval. I just don't understand what it is I'm supposed to feel." I don't understand how I'm to "feel" anything without actually touching it. I don't understand what it is I'm to be learning from this."

He had another exercise which he did frequently. It involved the words, "Where are you?" This one I understood. He simply wanted to know where each of us happened to be with our thoughts. When he turned the lights back on, he asked me, "Where are you? I asked, "Do you really want me to tell you the truth?" He said, "Certainly," so I proceeded to say that in my mind I was at home. I was thinking about the things I needed to do when I got home. The lawn needed to be mowed. The car needed to be washed. I said, "Sir, I apologize for interrupting the class but I'm confused. What does experiencing my belly button have to do with anything? I'm a grown man with a wife and two children and I didn't pay tuition to do this." To his credit, he didn't get upset at me. He thanked me for my honesty, although I never did understand what we were doing.

Know the Whole Book

One of my courses in graduate school was History of Education. I thought I knew about education and its history but having a course where the teacher is also the author of the textbook is another matter. The teacher in question had

They Call Me Doc

retired from teaching at the college level in the city of New York. The very first day of class he put the fear in all of us. He said, "Your final exam for this class will be a personal oral interview with me. Since I wrote the book, I have the right to ask any questions, so you'd better be prepared."

I immediately began reading, highlighting, and memorizing everything I thought would be asked. During the semester, I did fine in all the other work and thought I would be prepared for anything he would ask. As the semester was coming to a close, he once again reminded us of our oral interview with him. We had to make an appointment to see him outside of our regular class time. My interview was to be on a Saturday morning. He had told us to allow for a full hour of time. He also told us we were not to discuss what we talked about with any of the other students.

That Saturday morning that I was to meet him, I was a little anxious. What would he ask? Was I adequately prepared? His first name was Adolf and that was intimidating enough. I thought I should at least make a good impression so I put on a black suit with a red power tie, and a crisp white shirt.

When I entered his office, he was seated behind the desk. He was close to eighty years of age and had beautiful white hair. He motioned for me to be seated and then began to have a conversation with me. It went something like this:

"Ken, what do you do?" I responded that I was the principal of a church related school, teaching second and third grades and working in the church as the music and

They Call Me Doc

youth director. He responded that it was obvious I was very busy. Then he said, "Do you enjoy what you're doing?" I told him I did. What he said next was the shocker. "Thanks for coming in. Have a good day." I didn't know if I should hug him or kick him. I got up and left.

I honestly do not know if he did everyone in the class that way or not. I took him at his word that we were not to discuss our conversation with anyone. All I know is that I got a good grade and the irony of it all, I learned about the history of education. That may have been his motive. Is that a good method of teaching? You'll have to make that decision for yourself.

There are other events that could be told, such as "Pot poor-re or Potpourri," "Don't tell a dummy how to be saved," "He didn't know the gum was loaded," and "What's all the yelling about?" But they'll have to wait for another time. When you happen to be a teacher and a preacher, you're bound to have experiences that are humorous, sometimes even embarrassing, and sometimes even painful.

I've shared these with you for two basic reasons. First, students need to know that teachers are humans, too. They have emotions like everyone else. Second, you need to be able to laugh at yourself. While I have not included a sense of humor as one of the characteristics of being a good teacher, I believe it is.

Section Four

Educational Issues
The Christian and the Public Schools
Christianity and Psychology
Self-Concept and Children

They Call Me Doc

Educational Issues

Life is often filled with decisions that are hard to make. When I began writing this book, there were four things I wanted to include. I didn't want to write a complete autobiography, but I did want to include something about myself and my experiences as a teacher. I wanted to put in print the directions I have sensed in my educational career and ministry as a means of giving praise to the Lord. There have been too many of His confirmations for my experiences to have been an accident. I firmly believe He has led me all the way.

The second thing I wanted to do was point out what I believe to be some of the good characteristics, or attributes, all teachers should possess. Obviously, our greatest model is Jesus Christ and while Christian teachers should strive to emulate Him, there are others to be emulated as well.

The third thing I wanted to do was share some of the antics that have occurred along the way. It's been an enjoyable adventure and as a teacher and a minister I wanted you to be able to laugh with me at some of those experiences.

In the fourth section I wanted to be a little more philosophical and write about some educational issues I've experienced. For a time I wasn't sure I wanted to include this but the more I thought about it, the more convinced I became that I should. I know the biblical principle that says if you have a doubt about something don't do it, but there's another biblical principle that the Apostle Peter talks about. His principle is we should be ready to give an answer when we are asked about the hope we have in the Lord and for several years I have lived by that principle (1 Peter 3:15). I have three different messages using Peter's text that express my beliefs about why I believe in missions, why I am a Christian, and why I believe the Bible. I suppose my educational philosophy could be a message showing why I believe Christians can have a career, and a ministry, in a public school.

My life has literally been involved in education. I'd like to think I'm an educator, but I have never expressed my views, at least publicly or in print, about a Christian teacher who teaches in what some would call a secular society. I am very much aware that this is a point of controversy for some, but I have never really understood why; or maybe I have understood but didn't agree. There are too many illustrations in the Bible of people who ministered in societies that were far more corrupt than ours and yet they served. As I look at the life of Jesus, it seems to me He was teaching that we should infiltrate society, not be isolated from it.

During my educational/ministerial career, I have repeatedly been asked what I believe about a variety of issues. Three such issues seemed to crop up more than others. They are: (1) the Christian and the public school; (2) Psychology and Christianity; and (3) Children and their self-esteem.

THE CHRISTIAN AND THE PUBLIC SCHOOL

The twenty-three years I was privileged to serve on the faculty of Free Will Baptist Bible College were undoubtedly a highlight of my life. To quote a line from the pen of Charles Dickens, "It was the worst of time; it was the best of times."

They Call Me Doc

In my case, there were more best times than worst. The best times included having the opportunity to work and minister with some of the greatest people on earth. Being with students and watching them develop and become a success in their respective areas of education made the journey well worth it. I know former students today who have become school administrators in every level of education, including college. Others have become classroom teachers, counselors, and authors. Some have written materials that are being used by complete school districts. Some have positions with their local and state governments in departments of education. Some have become denominational leaders in their own right. To think I may have played a small part in their lives is humbling. The worst of times have been few and minor by comparison. Neither time, nor desire, permits me to describe them all, and some only indirectly had an impact on me.

I'm not sure about everything that is meant when the Bible says tribulation brings patience, and I'm even less sure if my "worst of times" experiences can be compared to tribulation. I do know there were some troublesome times, but I really doubt that they can be compared with tribulations that men and women of the Bible faced. Nor can they be compared with the hundreds of believers around the world today who know real tribulation and persecution.

Most of the issues in my educational experiences revolved around personalities rather than principles. Principles came to the forefront but there were strong personalities behind each one. Among the issues I experienced during my days as a faculty member of Free Will Baptist Bible College were: pastoral authority, the wine made by Jesus at the wedding in

They Call Me Doc

Cana of Galilee, and the issue of Christians and the public schools. Since my concern deals with Christians and the public schools, that's the only one I want to present here.

In the 1960's and beyond, across the denomination many pastors and churches were beginning to establish Christian schools as a part of their ministry. There were those who started with only a few students and utilized curricula known as Accelerated Christian Education, or simply A.C.E. In such schools students could work at their own rate of speed and even speed up the typical time frame for graduation. It was a system where a very small church could house a school on a limited budget and provide several grades at a time in one room. In most cases students were supervised by an individual known as a Monitor who would give personal help or instruction as needed. The churches who established schools this way are to be commended for their effort.

Other schools were being established with the more traditional approach of a self-contained classroom. Schools of this type would use a variety of curriculums, but most popular among them was a program established by the Pensacola Christian College known as ABeka. It was, and is, a program that stresses phonics as the key ingredient in teaching reading. Every subject is thoroughly integrated with Bible memorization and principles. Pensacola Christian College provided Teaching Clinics for both teachers and administrators who wanted to have certification from a Christian organization, although the certification was not recognized by some state departments of education for licensure. This is one of the main reasons why the administration of Free Will Baptist Bible College established a teacher education program. The objective was then, and still is, to have a recognized, accredited program that would lead to licensure by the Tennessee State Department of Education. It was believed then, and has since been proven, that other states would recognize, and reciprocate both the degree and licensure of graduates of Free Will Baptist Bible College.

No one can doubt the validity of churches beginning Christian schools. My disagreements have never been with that. Often, the growth in enrollment was hampered because of the lack of personnel available to teach. There simply were not enough teachers available to fill the classrooms.

Out of this growth of Christian schools, literally cropping up all over the Free Will Baptist denomination, there rose a philosophy with which I disagreed. My disagreement was with the philosophy, or belief, that was being promoted. I did not disagree with the personalities involved but with the principle they were expressing. Even now as I look back, I believe they thought they were doing the right thing. The belief that was being expressed became known as the Mandate Position.

To the best of my knowledge, the Mandate Position was comprised of three basic beliefs:

1. Christians who have a desire to teach should only teach in a Christian school

2. Christian parents should only send their children to a Christian school

3. The church has been given a scriptural mandate to

provide an education for children and the church should take priority over the government or state.

There may have been some other aspects involved, but these three seem to be at the heart of the issue. The public school, or as they were being called, Government School, should not be an option for Christians. Some of the proponents of this position believed, or at least stated, that for Christians to teach in a public school and Christian parents to enroll their children in a public school was actually sinful.

During this time frame, I was serving as the chairman of the teacher education faculty of Free Will Baptist Bible College. The college had been successful in achieving full accreditation by the Tennessee State Department of Education as well as full licensure for graduates. Besides serving as the chairman, I taught several classes in the teacher education curriculum and directed the student teaching program. In that area it was my responsibility to arrange for students to do student teaching, typically in the Metro Nashville Public Schools. Students hoping to graduate with a degree in teacher education and ultimately receive licensure had to follow the guidelines established by the Tennessee State Department of Education. That was a problem for those who were proponents of the Mandate Position.

If the Mandate Position was correct and Christians should only teach in Christian schools, why was the Bible College following standards established by the government? Was the Bible College encouraging graduates of the teacher education program to teach in the public schools? Did the teacher education curriculum make any provision to show the

They Call Me Doc

difference between Christian schools and the public schools? Could a student in the teacher education program do student teaching in a Christian school instead of a public school? These are only a few of the questions that were being raised. The whole concept was becoming a divisive issue.

I cannot speak for Mr. William Henry Oliver, or Dr. Douglas Simpson, the two men with whom I served to begin developing the teacher education program, but there was never a time when either of us, nor the Administration of Free Will Baptist Bible College, intended the teacher education program to become divisive. Our motive was to establish a program that would prepare students to be the best trained teachers they could be. We believed that a Christian should be trained in the Bible as well as other academic disciplines. We believed that any Christian who planned to be a teacher should be as well trained as, and even surpass, those who were trained in a secular environment. I would often say to students, "It's my responsibility to help you become the best teacher possible. It's up to you and the Lord to decide where that will be."

Such a philosophical attitude did not satisfy the proponents of the Mandate Position. It became a personal issue with me and a few of the proponents. One approached me and said, "Doc, I believe we agree. It's a matter of semantics. You believe that a Christian could have an influence in the public school, but don't you agree that a Christian teacher would have a greater influence in a Christian school?" I didn't have to think long about that so I responded, "No. There are situations where a Christian teacher in the public school could have a greater influence than he or she would in a Christian school." He didn't like

They Call Me Doc

that response and said, "I guess we really do disagree."

The situation seemed to get worse, at least in my opinion. On another occasion I was talking to a proponent of the Mandate Position who was a pastor. In our conversation he made this statement: "I will never have a deacon in any church I pastor whose children are in a public school." That prompted a lengthy discussion about what I felt was adding something to the qualifications of a deacon as taught by the Apostle Paul in both Titus chapter one and 1 Timothy chapter three. I reminded him that the Bible spoke against adding things to it.

A part of my disagreement with the Mandate Position revolved around the fact that some Christian schools, as good as they may be, are not equipped (particularly in those earlier days) to help students who may have special needs, sometimes referred to as handicapped, or students with physically, intellectually, or emotional needs. That prompted more discussion with others.

One personal friend who was on the side of the Mandate Position did, however, give me a phone call a few years later. His church sponsored a Christian school. He called to tell me he came to understand what I meant by saying some Christian schools could not handle the problems some students have. The day he called me, he had to recommend to a family in his school that they withdraw their student and put him in a public school that had the facility and the personnel the student needed. After he did that, he called me and said, "Doc, it hit me. If I believe it's wrong for Christian parents to enroll their children in a public school, I just helped a family do something wrong." I thanked him for his call and then said, "Are you going to tell your mandate friends about it?" He said, "Oh, no. I can't afford to do that," and then hung up.

When the Mandate Position was being urged, I had private conversations with several people on both sides of the issue, but I never developed any good reasons for my opposition. Through the years, with less emotion now, I have developed the reasons why I believe such a position is wrong.

It Is Unbiblical

That may be too strong for some to accept, but I believe I'm right. It's unbiblical for several reasons; mainly there are at least five illustrations in the Bible that seem to show God's people have been successful in using their influence in corrupt situations. Granted, the illustrations to some may only be historical and are not meant to be copied by us; but somehow I believe they are there to show us that the power of God can penetrate the worst of situations.

Moses

Most of you reading this will know the name Moses. You know his story. You know how the providence of God spared his life when other Hebrew boys were being killed. You know that Moses was actually educated in Egyptian schools. You know how God used Moses' influence to deliver the Jewish people from their years of bondage. Am I stretching it too far to say in our terms Moses was a believer and Egypt represented unbelievers? Was Pharaoh a tyrant and

They Call Me Doc

leader of a corrupt government? What if there had been no Moses? God could have risen up another leader instead and for that matter; God could have just as easily wiped Pharaoh off the face of the earth and done away with the whole problem. But for some reason God used a godly man to show a wicked society the power of God.

Joseph

Who can deny the influence of the life of Joseph in the land of Egypt? If you've forgotten about him, I suggest you go back and read chapters 37-50 of the book of Genesis. It's an amazing story of how God used a believer to influence a godless ruler and nation. God used Joseph to function in a secular government. The same questions asked about Moses could be asked about Joseph. Joseph's influence was so powerful he became second in command in the entire nation. Only Pharaoh himself had more power. With the help of God, Joseph saved a nation from economic ruin. As long as Joseph was in charge, the nation prospered. As vile and wicked as Egypt was, Pharaoh recognized there was something different about this "believer." There was a difference! Scripture tells us, *"And the Lord was with Joseph"* (Genesis 39:2); *"And his master saw that the Lord was with him"* (Genesis 39:3); *"But the Lord was with Joseph"* (Genesis 39:21); *"The Lord was with him"* (Genesis 39:23). In fact, some of the problems of the Children of Israel began after the death of Joseph. Again, Scripture says, *"Now there rose up a new king over Egypt, which knew not Joseph"* (Exodus 1:8). The sad truth is there was no one prepared to take Joseph's place.

They Call Me Doc

Daniel and the Three Hebrew Children

The stories I was told as a child about people like Moses, Joseph, Daniel, and the three Hebrew children still excite me. Daniel, Shadrach, Meshach, and Abednego were godly men serving in godless Babylon. Again, what if they had not been around? If you've forgotten about them, reread Daniel chapters 1-6. Let me remind you they were even educated by the corrupt government of Babylon! I would dare say that the governments of Egypt and Babylon were far more corrupt than anything we have ever faced, and yet God's people did what they could to combat the evil. Would it be stretching it to say Egypt and Babylon would have been worse had it not been for the godly men God had placed there?

The Great Commission

Any serious student of the Bible is familiar with what is called the Great Commission. It appears in Matthew 28:18-20; Mark 16:15; Luke 24:46-47; and Acts 1:8. I've always thought John 17:18 should be included as well. I was taught that the three aspects of the Great Commission are to preach, baptize, and teach. I have no problem with any of that. I believe it and have tried to practice it. My point, however, is this: what is it we are to be teaching as we are going to the ends of the world? There are those who have taught that this is the verse that gives the mandate because it states that we are to be teaching. But teaching what? The context makes it clear. As we are going to the ends of the world we are to be teaching the death, burial, and resurrection of Jesus Christ. As we preach about the Lord's coming to earth to save us from our sins, and baptize those who will accept Him, we are to teach them the things of God. The Great Commission in no way is saying we should be involved in reading, 'riting, and 'rithmetic.

Jesus Himself

To understand the life of Jesus, you must recognize there were three times in His life when nothing is said about Him. (1) From His birth until He was eight days old; (2) from eight days old until He was age twelve; and (3) from the age of twelve until the age of thirty. I find the silence to be very significant. His earthly parents brought him up as a typical Jewish boy. He was no doubt even educated like other Jewish boys His age. When Jesus began His earthly ministry, there are at least two times where He illustrates that believers must not be of the world, even though they are in the world. The first one is after His appearance as a boy of twelve years of age in the Jewish synagogue. The medical doctor Luke, in Luke 2:41-52, describes for us what Jesus did. Luke tells us that Jesus, as a young man, did four things: (1) He listened to people older than He was; (2) *He attended the church of His day;* (3) He submitted to His earthly parents; and (4) He grew in a normal fashion. I have put number two in italics to call attention to another passage when Jesus was a grown man. Luke states in Luke 4:16, *"And as his custom was he went into the synagogue on the Sabbath day."*

When you follow the life of Jesus, you recognize that He was keenly aware that the religious and political environments of His day were not what they should have been. He spoke against both of them, but He never isolated Himself from either of them. He warned His disciples about how they would be treated and it would not be with kindness. In Matthew 10:16 Jesus said, *"Behold I send you forth as sheep in the*

They Call Me Doc

midst of wolves." That's not a very promising future but He did not tell them not to go. Every student of the Bible knows sheep represent believers and wolves represent unbelievers. The rest of the verse says, *"Be...wise as serpents, and harmless as doves."* Again, they are not told not to go. Quite the contrary, they're told to go but to exercise caution and care. Where were they told to go? To a society that was wicked and corrupt. They were not to become like that society, but they were to go into it.

If the Great Commission has any meaning at all, it has to mean that believers are to go to as many people as they can. To say that believers are not to be involved in some of the same things as unbelievers, even in government, is to make the Great Commission useless. Don't forget that Jesus mingled with some of the worst of lifestyles.

On another occasion the Pharisees criticized Jesus because He dared to be with *"many publicans and sinners"* (Matthew 9:11). When the Pharisees asked about it Jesus replied, *"They that be whole need not a physician, but they that are sick"* (Matthew 9:12). Farther in that chapter Jesus gets very plain when He says, *"I am not come to call the righteous, but sinners to repentance"* (Matthew 9:13). In this same context Jesus said to the Pharisees, *"Go and learn what that meaneth"* (Matthew 9:13). That may be the most important part of the passage. A part of this must mean that believers are not to isolate themselves from the very people they're trying to influence.

During the earthly ministry of Jesus, He was constantly under the scrutiny of someone. There were those who were waiting for Him to slip up and make a mistake. Do you remember the incident with a coin? Jesus was asked if it was

They Call Me Doc

lawful to give money to the government. How did He respond? *"Show me a penny. Whose image and superscription hath it? They answered and said, Caesar's. And he said unto them, Render therefore unto Caesar the things which be Caesar's and unto God the things which be God's"* (Luke 20:24-25). That seems to be saying there is a place for the government in the lives of believers. The Apostle Paul echoes that same teaching in Romans 13:1-7.

It is Inconsistent

During the days when the Mandate Position was prevalent, I wanted to ask a question but didn't know exactly how to ask it. The question is: When did the mandate position become true? If it was a sin, or at least not proper, for Christians to refrain from sending students to public schools and refrain from teaching in one, when did that occur? If it has always been wrong, why did most of the proponents of the position attend public school in their childhood? Why did Christian parents not send their children to a private Christian school years ago? There seems to be two answers, if not more, to that question: there were very few Christian schools, if any, to send children to; and there never has been such a mandate. It could be argued that there was no need in years gone by for what we now know as the private Christian school, since many public schools still practiced Bible reading, prayer, and high standards of morality. I concede that observation, but I must confess I've wondered if we had put as much time and energy as parents and ministers into becoming involved with public education as we have in the Christian school movement, would things be different today? I don't know the answer to that.

They Call Me Doc

It's inconsistent because we don't hold that same standard for other areas of life. None of us when we need medical attention look only for a Christian doctor. I grant you, it's a comfort when your doctor happens to be a believer, but if I needed a heart transplant, I want to be sure the surgeon is qualified to operate on me even if he's an atheist. We don't look for a mechanic, dentist, grocery store, or Starbucks by asking if the owners are Christians. We certainly don't say that it's a sin, or inappropriate, for someone to serve in any branch of the armed forces. Quite the contrary. When someone does serve we applaud them for being patriotic. If they refuse to serve we call them a traitor.

I know what some will think. There's a difference between having a car fixed or buying groceries and having someone teaching your child's mind. The wrong person teaching your children can teach them the wrong thing, even for eternity, and once again, I will concede the difference. However, everything I continue to read and hear says the number one greatest influence in the lives of children is still their parents, not teachers.

I was fortunate in my elementary and high school days to have many Christian teachers. Through the years, and even today, I have personally known countless numbers of Christians who have an influence in the public school as well as in departments of education, both locally and statewide. In twenty years as an adjunct professor for Nashville State Community College, I have had several opportunities to influence students. I've prayed privately with them. I have counseled them in spiritual matters. I even performed a wedding for one couple. Not one time have I ever been told by those who hired me to stop. In the course of simple

They Call Me Doc

conversation with many friends who teach in public institutions in almost every grade from elementary to college, they report similar experiences.

Why is it that during a political campaign, believers get really excited when a candidate seems to have Christian values? We're hoping and praying that if they should win they can help make changes. Why, then, do we often make a Christian teacher in the public school feel guilty when they're trying to do the same thing? The Mandate Position, in my opinion, has done a grave injustice to both parents and teachers who either teach or place their children in a public school.

There was another reason I felt the mandate position was inconsistent. This reason relates to a form of classroom and curriculum which I mentioned earlier called Accelerated Christian Education, or A.C.E. I wrote an article about this at the request of the editor of what was then *Contact* magazine expressing my concerns, much to the dismay of some of those who were using A.C.E. I was familiar with it because my own children were in a Christian school at the time where this was being used.

However, it was not the A.C.E. curriculum itself that gave me concern. My concern was much different. The proponents of the Mandate Position were promoting the concept that government schools were not appropriate for Christians. While I disagreed with that, and still do, my concern arose when on an occasion I had an opportunity to visit the A.C.E. home office and headquarters in Texas. I knew one of their executives who had previously worked in a Free Will Baptist Church in Norfolk, Virginia at the same

They Call Me Doc

time I did. I was in Texas for another matter but took the opportunity to go and visit not only my friend, but to tour the facilities of A.C.E.

As I was being escorted through the facilities I learned that A.C.E. was not only publishing materials for Christian schools, but there was a division of their ministry that published materials for the public schools as well. That is, there were those public schools that because A.C.E.'s curriculum was devised so that an individual could work at his own pace, (also meaning Packet of Accelerated Christian Education), some public schools were using the A.C.E. packets to supplement those students who might either need extra attention because of an intellectual deficiency or because they were gifted and wanted to do more.

I have no problem with why the public schools were using A.C.E. material. I even commended those at the A.C.E. home office for making their materials available to them. In fact, I recently made a contact with them to verify that they are still producing materials for public schools and was delighted to learn they still are. I felt it was inconsistent for the proponents of the Mandate Position to state government schools should not be an option for Christians when public schools have the option to use some of the same materials as Christian schools.

It Has the Wrong Premise

The Mandate Position, at least in principle if not in practice, held that the government supported schools should not have the authority to tell what our children learn. They, the government schools, are not the ones that should be

They Call Me Doc

teaching our children. So far, so good. The Mandate Position farther stated that the mandate for the education of children was given to the church. That's where I had, and have, the problem. If I understand the Bible, neither the government, or state, nor the church has that authority. The authority to educate children is the responsibility of parents. They are the ones who ultimately make that decision. The parents are the ones who choose to home school, or to use a public school, or to send their children to a private non-Christian school or a Christian school. There have been those who used Deuteronomy 6:6-9 as evidence of having a mandate. I agree there is a mandate expressed in that passage, but it's not a mandate to the government or church. It's a mandate to the parents.

This is the issue that affected me the most during my days of serving on the faculty of Free Will Baptist Bible College. When I started teaching, my wife and I had two sons. A third one came later. All three of my sons attended a Christian school for a part of their education. It was a financial hardship at times, but God provided. As my sons grew older, I was faced with decisions to make. For a time two of them attended a Christian school at the same time. One, the oldest, had already begun giving thought to becoming a medical doctor. The Christian school he was attending, because of finances and personnel, was limited in the math and science courses. I knew those two areas were vital to the possibility of being accepted into a medical school down the road. The time came when Carolyn and I, along with our son, thought he should change schools. We enrolled him in a local high school that offered the courses he would need to continue preparation to possibly go to medical school.

They Call Me Doc

When he graduated from high school, he was still intent on being a medical doctor. He attended Free Will Baptist Bible College for three years in the teacher education program, transferred to another college in Nashville to get some pre-med classes, returned to Free Will Baptist Bible College for a fifth year and graduated with a teaching degree where he was licensed by the Tennessee State Department of Education to teach science, chemistry, physics, and biology. After graduation he taught for awhile in the Metro Nashville School system until he enrolled in medical school.

My second son had a different experience. While he was attending a Christian school, and unbeknown to me for a time, he sensed that God was calling him to be a preacher. When I learned of his interest I discouraged it for awhile because I wanted to be sure God was calling him and not me. He became convinced that was God's leading for his life. He remained and ultimately graduated from that Christian high school because we felt that was the best place to receive the training necessary for the ministry. After graduation from high school, he, too, attended and graduated from Free Will Baptist Bible College. Later he received a Master's Degree from Trevecca University and a doctorate from Oxford Graduate School and now is my pastor!

Son number three was keenly interested in music but was uncertain as to whether it should be in the secular field or in the Christian contemporary area. I offered him a challenge. One of the perks for being on the faculty at Free Will Baptist Bible College was that children of faculty members could receive free tuition. If they lived in the dormitory, you paid that expense. I told my son that since he was uncertain and since he could live at home and actually go to college at no

They Call Me Doc

expense, if he found a college that could match in a scholarship what the perk of free tuition would be, he could go to that college. He and his mother visited some schools but none could match my challenge, until he went to visit Austin Peay State University in Clarksville, Tennessee. They were known to have an excellent music program. He had met their music director when he attended a week-long camp called the Governor's School for the Arts. He had auditioned for a position at what was then Opryland U.S.A. to perform in a musical entitled, "I Hear America Singing." He was accepted in the musical and performed over 200 times. The Music Director from Austin Peay State University had written the Opryland program in which our son was employed.

His interview in Clarksville was very successful, in that he was offered not only an academic scholarship, but also enough funds to live off campus. After attending Austin Peay State University, he transferred to Belmont College in Nashville where he ultimately graduated and later returned and completed a Master's degree in Business Administration. The irony of all of this is that whatever success he has had in music has been almost exclusively in church music. He worked for several years for Lifeway, a ministry of the Southern Baptist Convention, in their music department assisting church choir directors with their music. The most recent project has been assisting song writer and publisher Greg Nelson in the rewriting of a hymn book for the Southern Baptist Convention, as well as writing children's songs for Vacation Bible School and other venues.

Why have I spent so much time going into the education of my three sons? Mainly because they were the target of some of the proponents of the Mandate Position. I was

They Call Me Doc

criticized for not sending my sons exclusively to Christian schools but I firmly believed then, and still believe, three things: (1) the education of my children was not the decision of the state or the church. It was exclusively that of my wife and me. (2) I was following what is the biblical mandate found in Proverbs 22:6, *"Train up a child in the way he should go, and when he is old, he will not depart from it."* Solomon is stating that parents have the obligation to help their children discover their God given gifts, talents, and abilities. Once you discern what those are, train, mold, discipline, and educate in that way so when the time is right, your children will do what God has ordained them to do. (3) If I had done any differently with either of my sons, they might not be doing what they are today, but to the glory of God, all three faithfully serve the Lord in their chosen pursuits.

It has been divisive

If the Scriptures teach anything, they teach that God's people should be united. The Psalmist said, *"Behold, how good and how pleasant it is for brethren to dwell together in unity"* (Psalm 133:1). The Apostle Paul echoed that same sentiment when he wrote, *"Endeavouring to keep the unity of the Spirit in the bond of peace"* (Ephesians 4:3). That word "endeavouring" carries the idea of being zealous, making haste, and giving diligence. The word "bond" carries the idea of being bound, or tied together. The picture is that of two or more prisoners being bound together so they cannot easily run away, but even if they do, they will still be together. But the bond with which believers are to be bound is not with chains, but with peace. Paul farther calls it the unity of faith in Ephesians 4:13.

I know I may be sadly misunderstood at this point, but I

They Call Me Doc

believe a tremendous amount of damage to the body of Christ has resulted from the Mandate Position. Believers have been divided; churches have been hurt; good godly, Christian men and women who are teaching in the public arena and using their influence for God have been made to feel inferior; and Christian fellowship among believers has been severed; a denomination has been divided. It would have been bad enough if it was a division between believers and unbelievers, but it's been a division between believers and fellow believers; a division between pastors; and a division between churches. That within itself should say something.

I will never know what prompted the Mandate Position. In some strange way I believe those who were involved, and continue to be, believed it was the right thing to do. I have purposely chosen not to mention people. I personally know many Christian people serving in the public school system. Some of them are in preschool, kindergarten, elementary, middle school, junior high, high school, college and beyond. Some are in county and city school board offices and state departments of education. Some serve as teachers, while others are administrators. Some are essential staff workers like janitors, nurses, cooks, and office staff. Whoever they are and wherever they are, one thing is certain: you never truly know the influence of a teacher. They impact eternity!

CHRISTIANITY AND PSYCHOLOGY

Since 1991 I have been employed as an adjunct professor for Nashville State Community College. I teach three subjects: Introduction to Psychology, Human Growth and Development, and Educational Psychology. Nashville State has campuses in Antioch, Cookeville, Dickson,

They Call Me Doc

Nashville, and Waverly, Tennessee. I have taught at the Cookeville, Dickson, and Nashville campuses. My educational preparation has allowed me this opportunity since I have a master's degree in Guidance and Counseling, a master's degree in Curriculum and Instruction, and a doctorate in Curriculum and Instruction. A minimum of a master's degree with at least eighteen hours in the disciplines of psychology and education is required.

Through the years I have been asked, "Why would a Christian want to teach in the secular field of psychology, particularly on a secular campus?" I have tried to be diplomatic about it but in my mind the question should be "Why not?" I don't understand why some people would consider the area of psychology to be off limits for a Christian.

By definition psychology is "the science that studies the human mind and behavior." What is it about that definition that would even prompt someone to ask why a Christian would be involved in psychology? A psychology textbook may expand on that by stating that psychology is the scientific study of the behavior of organisms, or the study of how living creatures are able to interact with their environment and each other, or (in its simplest form) what makes humanity tick. The meaning of psychology could even be expanded to say that it overlaps with other sciences like sociology, anthropology, physiology, and religion. But again, why would these things prohibit a Christian from having a career in psychology?

In my psychology classes I often state that psychology is not a curriculum; it's a way of life. You see psychology every

Educational Issues

They Call Me Doc

day in everyday experiences. You see it in politics, advertising, education, the media, religion, and relationships. It's a matter of seeking to understand the behaviors and mental processes of people. As simply as I know how, here is how I approach the subject of psychology and Christianity.

1. Psychology and Christianity provide information for daily living.

2. Psychology and Christianity suggest ways for humanity to be responsible citizens.

3. Psychology and Christianity give ideas and methods of how to be better people on the job, and in the family.

4. Psychology and Christianity teach the necessity of developing individuals to be the very best in all areas of life.

5. Psychology and Christianity provide information about what to expect in human growth and development.

Every psychology class I have ever taken as a student stressed that human growth and development is influenced by multi-directional, multi-contextual, multi-cultural, multi-disciplinary, and plasticity factors. That is, the human body and mind are a complex entity. To understand the behavior of mankind, you have to look at more than one aspect. You have to look at every facet of a person's life to fully understand that person. Understanding a person's behavior and mental processes begins with the kind of birth he or she

They Call Me Doc

experienced. Were there any complications? Was the person born prematurely? What number are they in their family? What about the genetic makeup? What about the culture around them?

A host of other questions could be listed, but the point is psychology and Christianity provides answers and let us know that growth and development are a normal process of life. The beginning student in the discipline of psychology will learn that humans are physical, social, emotional, and psychological beings.

Psychology and Christianity Do Have Differences.

It's at this point that I want to spend more time. And it's at this point that even on a secular campus I've had the opportunity to share how psychology and Christianity differ. In all of my classes I prepare a syllabus for students to follow along as I lecture. It has been amazing to me that when any subject about religion, morality, ethics, or Christianity comes up; students are more than willing to listen. Many of them are believers themselves and are encouraged and appreciative.

I will confess that there may not always be the same liberty that I enjoyed on the campus of Free Will Baptist Bible College, but I must also confess that sometimes the greater interests have come from the students on the secular campus. In my discussions, I point out the following differences, but I will spare you any commentary.

1. Christianity is based on the premise that all truth is God's truth.

They Call Me Doc

2. Christianity believes in absolutes, or the fact that truth can be known.

3. Christianity believes that the ultimate source of truth is found in God.

4. Christianity believes that truth may be found in divine creation and Scriptures.

5. Psychology cannot explain the purpose of human existence nor the meaning of life on earth.

6. Psychology cannot offer any hope for life after death.

7. Psychology cannot offer any real comfort in times of tragedy and grief.

8. Psychological truth is not on the same level with the truth of Scriptures.

Often my students will have a variety of cultural and religious backgrounds. It's not unusual to have a mixture of denominations, atheists, Jews, and Muslims. I point out in the areas of truth and morality that every religion has three things in common. They each have a founder, a book, and a code of ethics. Obviously, in Christianity the founder is Jesus Christ, the book is the Bible, and the basic code is the Ten Commandments. To the Jewish students it's Abraham and Moses, the Torah, and the Ten Commandments. To the Muslim students it's Allah, the Koran, and the code of ethics that every Muslim is to practice. I also point out that the irony of all this is that all three groups are at war over the same eastern geographical parts of the world.

They Call Me Doc

I also point out another factor; that whatever religion a person practices, or does not practice, there is a common denominator. It comes down to a matter of faith. It's a choice as to where the individual decides to place his faith. Even an atheist practices faith. He believes there is no God. Anytime you use the word "believe" you're stating your faith.

On one occasion I had a student who boldly told me he was an atheist. At the beginning of the first class he came up to me, dressed in the gothic style: solid black clothes, black fingernail polish, black lipstick, body piercings, and chains draped around his chest. I had never met him before but he told me he heard I was a minister and he wanted me to know up front I was not going to convert him. He sat on the front row.

During the course of the semester, he politely asked questions and I responded with the same politeness. As the semester was drawing to a close, I asked him to remain after class for a moment. I then said something like, "You know, even though you say you're an atheist and I say I'm a Christian, we do have a similarity." He didn't quite understand so I continued. "Just suppose when I die I find out that everything I have believed about the Bible, Christ, and heaven is not true. Suppose there is no heaven or hell. There is no such thing as eternity. If when I die I find out I have been wrong, it won't hurt me to have believed what I have believed. But suppose when you die, and you find out there is a God, and heaven and hell are real, and there is an eternity, you'll have a big problem. Are you willing to take that risk? It boils down to a matter of faith. You say you don't believe in God. I say I do. The word believe is an act of faith." He thanked me for my thoughts and before the

They Call Me Doc

semester was over he told me I had almost convinced him there is a God, but he wasn't ready yet to really admit it. Why do I teach psychology in a secular institution? Because, like my teacher at Middle Tennessee State University who lectured to the class about why he was a Christian said, if I don't some may never hear the truth.

Psychology teaches that humans are emotional, social, physical, and intellectual beings. I take it a step farther and add the spiritual. In actuality Christianity is far greater because it has better answers. When psychology says that humans do what they do because of being mistreated or having a bad environment, Christianity says humans do what they do because they're sinful. Psychology seeks to change a person's environment and culture; Christianity seeks to change a person's character. Psychology has no hope to offer in this life or the life to come. Christianity offers both. Psychology says that humans are basically good. Christianity does recognize that even sinful people have a quality of goodness but are depraved and in need of redemption.

It's interesting, when you study the life of Jesus, that His very life demonstrates all the areas of psychological and human growth and development. Luke puts it this way: *"And Jesus increased in wisdom and stature, and in favor with God and man"* (Luke 2:52). Look at it closely. Increased: He continued to develop; wisdom: intellect and common sense; stature: physical growth; favor with God: spiritual; and favor with man: social. His emotional characteristics are seen throughout His ministry when He cried, had compassion, and displayed anger and frustration.

They Call Me Doc

Self-Concept and Children

I don't know the times I have been asked, "How do you build a good self-concept in the life of a child?" This question is the most difficult for me to answer. I love children and teenagers, but I'm not a child psychologist. My wife and I have raised three sons but I still feel somewhat inadequate in telling others how to raise their children. I have spoken at literally hundreds of family seminars and conferences and almost without exception the topic that people want help on the most has been in the area of raising their children.

Part of the difficulty in answering this question relates to the tension it brings between psychology and Christianity. I will be the first to admit that it's possible to go to the extreme and put too much emphasis on psychology, even to the point of overlooking the spiritual. As a student of psychology I have read men like Sigmund Freud, B.F. Skinner, Jean Piaget, Carl Rogers, Erik Erickson, Abraham Maslow and others. I have also read Christian authors like James Dobson, Paul Meier, Kevin Leman, and Frank Minirth. Obviously, I lean more toward the Christian authors, but that doesn't mean something cannot be learned from the secular viewpoints.

In answering this question I want to be more practical than psychological. I don't want to bog you down with technicalities and psychological jargon. I would like to approach this as if you and I were privileged to have a face to face conversation, not as professionals but as concerned parents. In presenting my answers, illustrations may be used from my own family since I'm more comfortable, and familiar, with them. Hopefully, you can make applications to

They Call Me Doc

your situation. There are four words I want to use that have been a tremendous help to me. They are: acceptance, attitudes, appreciation, and affection.

Acceptance

I firmly believe that life begins at conception. There is life in the womb prior to the actual moment of birth. That's a matter of logic and science. If there is no life in the womb, there is no growth, but every mother knows there is growth going on. They simply look in a mirror and notice that their own bodies are growing. There are three areas of acceptance that are vital to the development of a good self-concept in the lives of children. They are: (1) the gender of your child; (2) the individuality of your child; and (3) the abilities of your child.

The Gender of Your Child

Do you remember when your first child was born? During those nine months of expectancy you waited with impatience. You picked out a name and checked to be sure the initials didn't spell something obscene. You may have painted the room blue or pink only to have to repaint it when the baby was born. The clothes you got at the baby shower were for the wrong sex so you took them back. Parents today have an advantage over those of us whose children are older. Our children were born before ultra-sound and 3-D imaging of the baby in the womb. Today, parents are able to know the gender of the baby before birth. But here's my point. You may have wanted a boy, but you got her. You wanted a girl but you got him. If you don't accept the gender of your child, the child comes into the world already at a

They Call Me Doc

disadvantage. There is scientific evidence that children in the womb can detect your feelings, tone of voice, and attitude. They know if you really want them.

Some of you will find this hard to believe but in my teaching career, I have had five different students tell me they actually remember when they were in their mother's womb. All five have been at different times. When I have questioned them about it they have made comments like they remember feeling the inside of the body of their mother, or remember an event that took place. I have stated things like, "Do you really remember or did you hear your mother talk about it so much, you think you remember?" Almost every time their response has been something like, "No. I told my mother things she didn't know anyone knew but her."

Before you mark them off, let me remind you of a story in the Bible. It's the story of two women who were relatives. Their names were Elizabeth and Mary. Elizabeth was expecting a baby boy, whom we know as John the Baptist. Mary was expecting Jesus. Mary went to visit Elizabeth and when Mary came into the home of Elizabeth, when Elizabeth heard the voice of Mary, her baby jumped in her womb (Luke 1:39-44). He didn't just jump or move like a normal child would. He "jumped for joy." The hearing may have come from Elizabeth but the emotion of joy was his own.

The Individuality of Your Child

Frequently we say that all children are different. However, it's been my observation that we don't really believe this. We say they are different but then we want them all to act alike, we want them to act like us. It's not too difficult to accept a

They Call Me Doc

child's individuality if there's only one child in the family, although even then the child should not be expected to be like his parents. The harder part comes when you have more than one child in the family. I can assure you, they will not act alike, and they shouldn't. They are different. They have different emotions. They may be taller or shorter.

I remember growing up as a preacher's kid. As I got older, and went to high school, teachers would compare me to my older brother. Even later I was always being compared to Raymond and Winona, my parents. There was a time when I resented that. I didn't want to be known as "Raymond and Winona's boy." I wanted to be known for myself. I'm not condoning the rebellion I later demonstrated, but I want you to understand that children are different and they want to be recognized for who they are, not just by the family they're in.

Did you ever go to school and hear a teacher say, "Why don't you make good grades like your sister?" or "Why don't you behave like your daddy?" or maybe "Why do you behave like your daddy?" I remember, in my early days of teaching, I would recognize a student's last name on the class roll and realize I knew his parents, so I would make some comment about it. My motive was to be personable until I began to realize they might not want to be reminded of their parents. They want to be recognized for who they are. I soon stopped that practice. One secular psychologist by the name of Alfred Adler has a theory known as birth order. He believes the number you are in your family determines your personality. I can't say I completely agree with it, but I do understand his premise. Children are different and want to be treated that way.

They Call Me Doc

The Abilities of Your Child

This is closely related to accepting your child's individuality. The difference is this: accepting a children's individuality is to accept them as people; accepting their abilities is to accept what they can do and want to become. This is often demonstrated in the area of athletics. I have often said I would coach a Little League ball team under one condition: mom and dad sign a contract never to come to the games. I say that because I've been to too many athletic games where children are expected to act like professionals. They're expected to play like adults. They're expected to play beyond their physical abilities.

Let me go farther. Suppose you want your son to be a famous football player for your favorite college or professional team. But suppose he doesn't want to play football. He wants to play the violin. "Wait a minute. No son of mine is going to play a violin. That's for sissies." Who said so? I've seen it over and over again where parents try to relive their dreams in the lives of their children but it just doesn't work. I've had students come to my office many times and say something like this: "Doc, I would be in the ministry, but it's going to be an argument when I get home. Daddy wants me to come back home and work with him in his business" or "My parents are afraid I'm going to marry a preacher or a missionary and they don't want me to do that."

Parents, please take your hands off the lives of your children. Sure, give them guidance and directions but let them know you are willing for them to follow whatever and wherever the Lord may lead them. Go back and read Proverbs 22:6. Help your children find their God-given abilities and mold, educate, and direct in that way. Accept their gender; accept their individuality; and accept their abilities.

Attitudes

Attitudes are caught more than they're taught. What you do say far more than what you say. The old adage that says, "Don't do as I do, do as I say" never has been a good idea. The attitudes you display in front of your children are powerful. Another secular psychologist by the name of Erik Erickson has a theory known as Psychosocial Development in which he points out that positive attitudes can produce positive results and negative attitudes can produce negative results. Again, I don't accept everything he says, but he does have a point that needs to be tempered by balance. Even in the field of business, Kenneth Blanchard has written a little book entitled *The One Minute Manager* in which he points out, among other things, that people will work for less money when they know they are being appreciated. In other words, the attitude of their boss can bring about productivity or loss.

I would like to suggest four attitudes that parents need to guard against in developing a good self-concept in their children. They are: attitude about themselves; attitude about school; attitude about life; and attitude about church.

Attitude about Themselves

What you think of your children is typically what they think of themselves. My wife and I established a policy in our home when our boys were small. We did not, nor did we allow them, to call each other "dummy," "meathead,"

They Call Me Doc

"turkey," "stupid," or any other derogatory term. That belittles what God called good when He made man. Even an unsaved person is made in the image of God and deserves to be treated that way.

I'm confident that those of you reading this will agree with me that physical and sexual abuse of children is wrong. If you're like I am, it might make you mad when you hear about such cases. But there's another abuse far worse than physical and sexual abuse. It's emotional abuse. As bad as physical and sexual abuse may be, the scars they cause will heal with time. When a child has a constant diet of verbal abuse or being constantly put down, it leaves emotional scars that seldom, if ever, heal.

Attitude about School

If you're a teacher like I am, that gives you an advantage over other parents. We have to get up to go to school as well as our children. If you think it's rough being a student and facing teachers early in the morning, try being the teacher who has to face students! I remember those days very vividly when I would go and wake up my boys to go to school. Monday through Friday, they would have a hard time getting up, but on Saturday, the Road Runner would wake them up, with no problem. Saturday morning may have been the only day to sleep in but that's the day they would get up the earliest and want breakfast.

I remember going to their bedrooms and saying, "Get up boys. It's time to get ready for school." Sometimes their response would be, "Daddy, I don't want to go to school today." That's when I would say, "I don't want to go either so unless you're sick, you might as well get up. The attitude you wake up with will determine how well you do, so get up and get ready."

How you respond to your child's teacher and homework is also important. If your child starts bad-mouthing his teacher and you say something like, "Who are you talking about?" and he says, "That old Miss So-and-So" and you say, "You mean to tell me she's still there? She was there when I went to that school." Your child may go to school the next day and tell his teacher you said she was too old to be there. You didn't say those exact words, but you implied it with your comment. Or take the issue about homework. You look at what your child has to do and you say something like, "Why do you have to that? Why don't they teach you like they used to teach me?"

Every teacher knows that often they have to deal with the negatives that parents consciously or unconsciously instill in children. Today's teachers have other problems more serious than those in my elementary school days. In my day it was obvious that teachers and parents were on the same page. Both of them wanted children to get a good education. Both knew the importance of proper discipline. In fact, in my day if you got a paddling at school, which I did, you got another when you got home, which I did, because you got one at school. Not so today. Some parents will bring lawsuits against teachers if they don't like their method of teaching and discipline.

Take another issue. What does it say to children when fathers don't attend PTA meetings? Is it possible that a child gets an attitude that education must not be very important if

They Call Me Doc

daddy doesn't come to such meetings? I used to tell students who were planning to be teachers that they could retire as millionaires if they could figure out how to get parents who really need to come to parent-teacher conferences and PTA to attend. Typically, the parents who do come have children who are usually doing well.

Attitude about Life

If you are not a teacher by profession, let me assure you that you are still a teacher. You teach by example. You teach by what you say and do. You teach by what you don't say and don't do. What you think and how you act about the local police, politicians, other races, and other people influences the attitudes of your children. When I taught on the elementary levels I could often tell during an election year who the parents of my students were going to vote for. The children would say something negative about a politician that I know they didn't understand. They were simply parroting what they heard at home.

Something as simple as taking your child to the doctor, can be an opportunity to demonstrate and develop a good attitude. Every parent has had the experience of taking a child's temperature and discovering the child has a fever. If the fever continues, more than likely you will take your child to the doctor. If you go to the doctor with a child running a fever, you know the child will probably get a shot, so you start preparing yourself and your child. You might say something like, "Honey, do you want to go and see a nice man today?" Your child may respond, "Is he going to hurt me?" To which you may respond, "No, precious. I wouldn't let anyone hurt my baby," and your child believes you.

They Call Me Doc

At the doctor's office, you finally get in to see him. Your child is sitting on a table, or in your lap, not expecting anything to hurt. The doctor takes a depressor and looks down your child's throat, in his eyes and ears and then tells his nurse to get ready for an injection. Again, your child is very calm because he's not expecting anything to hurt, but all of a sudden the doctor jabs him in the arm and your child lets out a war whoop for the entire office to hear. You grab him and say, "Did that old, mean doctor hurt you?" You know why you said that? You lied and had to defend yourself. You said your child wouldn't get hurt and he did.

You may think I'm being extreme about this, but I firmly believe a child can figure it out. If you lied about that, what else might you be lying about? Tell the truth. Tell a child that he might get a shot, and, yes, it might hurt for awhile, but he'll get over it. You're not only developing an attitude in the mind of a child about his doctor, you're developing an attitude of trust in the mind of your child towards you. If you don't believe me, the next time your child has to get a shot, try telling the truth and see if it doesn't change things. Often, when a child knows he will get a shot, it doesn't hurt as much because he's expecting it to hurt.

Attitude about Church

"Get up kids. It's Sunday and we have to go to church. I don't want the pastor calling here tomorrow and asking where we were. Get up!" The family gets up and goes to church. When they get home, they may be served "roast preacher" for dinner when family members start talking about how boring and long the sermon was. I wish I was making that scenario up, but I'm afraid I'm not.

They Call Me Doc

An even worse scenario is when a young man may sense God is calling him to the ministry. His father may say, "Son, that's well and good, but you probably won't make a lot of money doing that." That may be true about the money, but that's my point. Too often we make money the value to follow instead of obedience. I must confess that I have attended some church meetings where good people disagreed over what I thought were insignificant issues and I wondered what the younger generations thought. Is it possible that sometimes a local church and a denomination can actually drive people away from the very thing we want them to love? I'm afraid so.

I certainly believe that the Bible is true. All of it! I have no doubt about it. But I also believe there are some issues in the Bible that should not be used as a test of fellowship. There's enough in the Bible for us to agree on without dividing ourselves into separate camps. Quite frankly, the older I get, the less some things mean to me. The older I get the more I realize I don't know as much as I thought I did. In some ways I wish I could go back to my younger days and apologize for some of the things I preached in such a dogmatic, and probably offensive, way.

There's just too much at stake in the raising of our children to make issues over things that none of us may really know for sure. I have come to the conclusion that I could be wrong about some things, but I have also come to the conclusion there are two things I firmly believe and as long as my fellow Christians believe them too, I'm going to fellowship and rejoice with them. What are those two things? The Bible is true and Jesus Christ is the only way to heaven. Beyond that, I'm going to agree to disagree with kindness and respect about other matters. I hope you will join me.

Appreciation

In case you've lost sight of what this section is about, let me remind you. The topic at hand relates to building self-esteem in the lives of children. You build self-esteem by accepting your children in three areas: their gender, their individuality, and their abilities. You build self-esteem by developing and demonstrating a good attitude in four areas: what you think about your child, what you think about education, what you think about life, and what you think about church.

The third word that, to me, helps in the development of self-esteem is the word appreciation. By appreciation, I mean two things. There is a negative aspect, and there is a positive aspect. The negative aspect means there are times when you simply have to say "No." It's a foolish parent who lets children make some decisions on their own. When you say no, the child may not fully understand and even if you try to explain your negative response, they still may not get it. That's why there are times when the only answer you can give a child is, "Because I said so." That's not in keeping with present day child psychology and it's certainly not politically correct.

You are the parent and that within itself gives you the authority to make decisions. That doesn't mean that as children get older they shouldn't be allowed to have some choices, but even then the choices should meet with your approval. Children should be given the opportunity to make decisions while you are there to help. Let me illustrate that

They Call Me Doc

from something we did in our family.

When all three of our sons were at home and still very young, their mother would often buy all the Christmas gifts. She would then put a label on each of the packages with the name of each boy and who the package was from. On Christmas morning when they opened their gifts, you would hear them say, "What did I get you?" In other words, since their mother bought the gifts, they didn't know what they bought each other.

We changed that and started giving them a prescribed amount of money. We would then tell them they had to spend what we gave them on gifts for each of their brothers and their mother and dad. They could not buy some little gadget and spend the rest of the money on themselves. They had to spend all the money on the family. That began a very humorous tradition. But the importance of it is the fact they learned how to budget their own money. They had to make decisions as to what to buy.

On the positive side, children need to know they are appreciated, not because of what they do but because of who they are. Dr. James Dobson of Focus on the Family calls this the gold and silver coins of worth. Some children are only appreciated if they are good athletes or make good grades. In comparison to the majority of students in school, not everyone can be athletic or intelligent; not all students are talented or good looking. What Dobson is saying is that not all children are sports minded, intelligent, talented, or beautiful, but they still have worth and value.

Here is where I have a little hesitation in expressing my

They Call Me Doc

feelings because I don't want anyone to think my wife and I were perfect parents. We were not, but we did try to let our boys know we appreciated them. It's the obligation of every parent to provide the necessities of life like food, shelter, clothing, safety, and education. Showing appreciation goes beyond these things. To illustrate what we did is risky, but to be sure you get my point, I will illustrate.

When our boys started school in the first grade, we literally told them we didn't care what kind of grades they made. They were expected to do their best, but if they honestly did their best and made a failing grade, we did not reprimand them. If they goofed off or didn't try, that was a different matter and appropriate measures were taken to remedy that.

To prove we meant what we said, we developed a plan that quite honestly I don't know where it came from. When report cards were brought home, it was understood that was a meal ticket for the family to go out for supper. If only one brought a report card home the entire family still went out. It made it easier when all three got report cards on the same day. When we went to supper, they had the privilege of ordering anything from the menu they wanted, including dessert. There were other times when they were much younger that their mother would order for them, but not on report card day. You must understand, however, that I selected the restaurants. That's important to remember. This was our way of letting them know we appreciated them

Some parents choose to give their children a dollar for every A on the report card. I don't think that's a good idea because some children cannot make A's and, unfortunately,

They Call Me Doc

some cheat to get them and if you give them money for making a grade they didn't deserve, you're rewarding cheating. To give money only for good grades is to say you only appreciate them because of their intelligence. The Biblical concept is to reward faithfulness, not accomplishment. We practiced the report card concept from the first grade through high school graduation. I confess it was costly, but, looking back, it's been worth it.

As the boys got older, even though we still practiced the report card routine, we did something else when each became a teenager. Remember, on report card day, I would choose the restaurant. On the thirteenth birthday, the birthday person chose the restaurant, and again the entire family went to supper. That's even more expensive, but worth it. Our oldest son chose a rather up-scale restaurant that was actually owned at the time by the Shoney's franchise. The cost of the meal for five people was about $35-$40 which is not bad by today's economy but that was thirty-two years ago!

Our second son reminded me he was to pick the restaurant for his thirteenth birthday. When I asked him where he wanted to go he said, "The Barn." The Barn is a dinner theatre west of Nashville that serves a full buffet and then you are entertained by either a musical, a mystery drama, or a comedy. I told him that would be fine, but I had to check to see what would be playing. I wasn't taking the family to see something inappropriate. He understood. My wife then asked me, "Do you know how much that costs?" I told her I did not but I would find out.

I called to make the reservations and discovered the cost was twelve dollars per person which would have been a total

They Call Me Doc

of $60 not including any tips. Again, not too bad for a family of five in today's economy but, again, go back thirty-five years ago and you'll see the difference. I did receive a discount of $2.00 because the youngest boy was under the age of twelve. The total bill was still between $65 and $70.

When our third son became a teenager, I learned he was encouraged by his older brothers to sock it to his dad. He planned for two years where he wanted to go. He chose one of the most exclusive and expensive restaurants in Nashville. The total bill exceeded the other two previous meals combined and then some. In fact, it would have cost $25 more if I had paid for the dessert. The owner of the restaurant made a visit to every table and when he got to our table he asked if this was a special occasion, I told him what it was. He liked the idea and graciously ordered dessert for all five of us at no charge.

After this last birthday bash was over and we sat around the table, my boys looked at me and said, "Daddy, what are you going to do now? You don't have any more children to be thirteen." I looked at them and said, "Rejoice." We talked some more and then my wife and I made a promise to each of them. When our sons' children get to be teenagers, we will take the birthday person and each one in their family to whatever restaurant the birthday person wants to attend. We have ten grandchildren! As of this writing, four of them have become teenagers and all four have selected The Barn, which is now $50 per person.

You may be thinking two things. First, I didn't know Christian school teachers and preachers made that kind of money. Believe me, they don't. Secondly, it seems you're

They Call Me Doc

trying to buy your children. That couldn't be farther from the truth. Yes, it has been expensive but stop and think about it. How many times are your children thirteen? Have you stopped to realize what has been happening at each of these events? The families have been together to establish some wonderful traditions. A good self-concept comes from a loving family! There's something else you need to know. I'd rather give a cashier money than to give it to a judge to get a child out of jail. Yes, it's been expensive, but I'd rather call it an investment, an investment in the lives of my children. An investment in their value to me and their mother. It's a matter of perspective. I know many families who spend far more on cigarettes and other tobacco products, as well as a host of other insignificant items. But as for me, if I'm going to "blow" my money, I'd rather blow it on my boys and grandchildren.

Affection

The word affection, obviously, means the demonstration of love. But how do you demonstrate love as your children get older? When they are young you can pick them up and hug them. You can hold them and rock them in your lap. Try that when they're bigger and taller than you. I don't know how to show love to girls in a family because all of our children are boys, and I've been told by parents who have girls that showing love to girls is definitely different. I have learned some things about demonstrating love, particularly to teenagers, that are very important in the developing of a good self-concept.

They Call Me Doc

Demonstrating love means attending their school functions

That's not always easy or convenient, but it must be done. I cannot tell you the times my wife and I have attended high school football games to see two boys march in the marching band. I cannot tell you how boring it may sometimes be to attend a music concert to listen to music you don't even like. I cannot tell you how many basketball games we have attended. But in every one of these situations, it has paid off to go.

I have to admit that I regret the few times I let other things interfere with what my sons were involved with in school. I let preaching engagements interfere with a few such events, and as I look back, it was wrong to do that. I have since come to the conclusion that a minister's greatest ministry is to his family and children, not his church or preaching ministry.

Demonstrating love means you have to let your children go.

That is extremely hard. When I say letting your children go, I'm not just referring to their getting married and leaving home. The Scriptures make it very plain that when someone gets married they are to leave mother and father (Genesis 2:24). Getting married is relatively the easiest part of all. Letting them go means letting them form their own ideas, values, and opinions. I certainly don't mean in the sense of allowing them to do things immoral. I'm referring to things like differences of opinions about music, clothing, food, careers, and host of other topics.

They Call Me Doc

Demonstrating love means your children may not be like you.

That may not be bad. Every family has its differences of opinions on a variety of subjects. When your children are small, they may not know some of the things you know, but as they get older, they begin to achieve more knowledge and may come to conclusions different from yours. They may have a different taste in foods. They may not even be as strict on their own children as you were on them, but you have to let them go.

Demonstrating love recognizes that children will be different in their emotions.

Some parents are more demonstrative in the outward affections they display; others are more reserved. Just because one child may hug and kiss his parents doesn't mean he loves you more than a child who doesn't do that as frequently. And just because one child may not hug as frequently doesn't mean he loves you less. Love recognizes there will always be differences.

Demonstrating love means when your child gets married, he has a new set of priorities.

There will come a time when your own children will not spend Christmas or Thanksgiving with you. Granted, I believe your children still have the responsibility to keep the lines of communication crystal clear regardless of whom they marry, but learn to give them some room.

How do you develop a good self-concept in the lives of

They Call Me Doc

children? Accept them. Accept their gender, their individuality, and their abilities. Develop good attitudes by demonstrating your attitude regarding them as people with worth and value; demonstrate your good attitude about education, life itself, and your church. Show them appreciation by going above and beyond what is expected of you. Don't hesitate being negative when they need to be corrected but balance that with a good measure of honest and sincere praise. Shower them with affections but recognize that more than likely they will one day leave home and start a family of their own.

Years ago *Reader's Digest* magazine produced an interesting article stating that raising children is very much like holding a bar of soap. When you get in the shower and get your soap wet, and let it just lie in your wet hand, it might slip out and fall to the floor; if you grip it too tightly it could still squirt out of your hand. You have to learn how much pressure to put on the soap to use it.

The same is true with a child. Too many parents don't put any grip at all on their children and let them do what they want. Proverbs 29:15, states *"A child left to himself bringeth his mother to shame."* In other words when there are no restraints given to a child, he may possibly embarrass his parents and make a fool of himself. On the other hand, Paul says, *"Fathers, provoke not your children to anger, lest they be discouraged"* (Colossians 3:21). The word "provoke" carries the idea of stirring up the emotion of anger in the life of a child. The word "discouraged" carries the idea of taking away the spirit of the child.

The application is that you can have too many restraints

and actually drive a child away from the very thing you want him to love. It's been my observation that in many Bible-believing, fundamental churches and homes; parents are more often too strict than they are too lenient. Too often we put children under too many rules and regulations to the point we may drive them away.

Go back to the bar of wet soap. Just as you have to learn how much pressure to put on the soap to use it, you have to learn how much pressure to put on children. Some will need more pressure than others but all need a measure of restraint.

They Call Me Doc

Closing Comments

I began this book with a short autobiographical journey. It seems I've come full circle and will end that way as well. I've had my share of heartaches in the ministry. I've had embarrassing things happen in the classroom, at weddings and funerals. I've had those times of disagreements that should never have separated Christian fellowship. I've known what it was for fellow Christians to sever relationships over things non-important, but fail to deal with issues that were. I've known what it was to feel disappointments over promotions you were hoping to get but they went to someone else. I've felt the pain in my heart when fellow Christians bring personal accusations that cut right through you. I've known the sick feeling you get in the pit of your stomach when a denomination seems to major on minors and minor on majors. I've known what it is to have a threatening phone call about not going to your office. I've known what it's like to go to that office only to find it had been ransacked.

What would it accomplish to go into those? I remember Dr. L. C. Johnson when he served as the President of Free Will Baptist Bible College saying something like this: "You don't serve God because you love people. You serve God because you love God. If you serve God because you love people, you'll quit. If you serve God because you love Him, you'll keep going. People will disappoint you, but God won't." My desire is to keep on going, and going, and going.

If you're one of my former students and a teacher as well, thanks for making this journey an enjoyable one. If you're still teaching, I wish you the best of everything. Hang in there. If you're a former student but have never taught, you

They Call Me Doc

don't know what you've missed. If I met you at a youth camp, family conference, your local church or wherever, you have enriched my life. If sometime in the future you see me, I hope you'll stop and talk. And like so many of my students, you're more than welcome to call me "Doc."

Ken Riggs (kennethriggs2001@hotmail.com)

They Call Me Doc